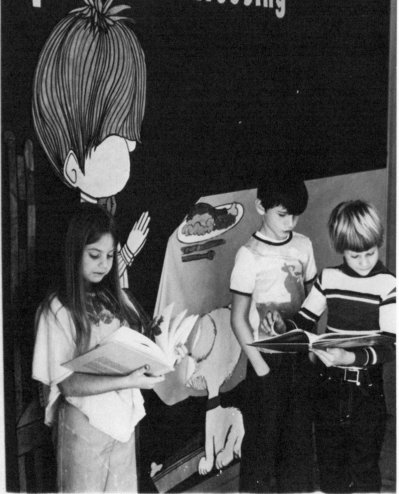

CELEBRATING
WITH BOOKS

WITHDRAWN

by

NANCY POLETTE

and

MARJORIE HAMLIN

*Line drawings by
Patricia Gilman*

The Scarecrow Press, Inc.

Metuchen, N.J.   1977

Photo credits: Frontispiece and photo on p. 43
courtesy of Pattonville School District; photo on
page 87, courtesy of Principia School, St. Louis
Co., Missouri.

Library of Congress Cataloging in Publication Data

Polette, Nancy.
  Celebrating with books.

  Includes bibliographies and index.
  1. Children's literature--Bibliography. 2. Holidays
--Juvenile literature--Bibliography. I. Hamlin,
Marjorie, joint author. II. Title.
Z1037.9.P64   028.52   [PN1009.A1]   77-3862
ISBN 0-8108-1032-8

CONTENTS

ACKNOWLEDGMENTS

The authors are indebted to Nan Borchert for the primary and pre-school activities developed to accompany books published by Charles Scribner's Sons and to the publisher for permission to reproduce art activities based on the illustrations in these books.

INTRODUCTION

A Recipe for Holiday Stew

Take: One forthcoming holiday

Mix with: 30 excited children

Add: An abundance of challenging, meaningful, heart-
             expanding, mind-stretching, creative and fun-
             filled books

Blend together well.

Result: A mixture that will enable children to obtain a
             view of life which is inaccessible in any other
             way and to savor special moments which are
             worth saving forever!

    Holidays offer the teacher an appealing array of books
which can catapult a classroom into continual mind-expanding
activities and learning experiences that are fun. These experiences can enhance the interior of any classroom. The
views afforded by challenging, eye-opening, mind-stretching
books can knock down any walls or restrictions. And they
are all waiting in libraries, pulsating with life and stimula-
tion. Open the covers and discover anew for yourself. Bring
them to your children. Fill your classroom with those books
which can bring holidays and the people who made them or
parade in them to life. You CAN lure children to books by
reading aloud, showing your interest, your excitement in what
you are reading and learning.

    We all respond better to "learning" than to being
"taught"! Sharing fun and stimulating books promotes learning effortlessly. The activities suggested in Celebrating with
Books will help you to direct your children with a "spoonful
of sugar" rather than a required pill. Imagine the reaction

in a primary classroom where a teacher announces, "Since
next week is Abraham Lincoln's birthday, today we are going
to start learning about his life. " Obviously she plans to
"teach" the children about him. In another classroom, a
teacher asks, "Would you like to go to a birthday party next
week? Guess who is having one?" After the answer "Lincoln" has emerged, she can pursue the idea with, "Shall we
give him a party here in our classroom? How shall we do
it? What would he like to see? What could we do for him?
Shall we find out?" The teacher is already well supplied
with a number of books on Lincoln, or suggests that the class
go to the library to find all that they can in preparation for
the event. The best finds are chosen to read aloud. The
more the class knows about this man, the better party they
will be prepared to offer him. Celebrating with Books will
lead you to a variety of ideas which the books can promote
for this holiday and for the many others which are included.

The nearing of U. N. Day can promote "flying carpets"
(books) which will take the class all over the world. The
activities which you will find herein can jet the children home
again with a deeper understanding of their world and those
who inhabit it.

The books on Christmas and Hanukkah might be considered "gifts" to Jews and Christians alike as they build the
children's appreciation of each other's traditions, history,
and mythology. What better gift to the world than more tolerance and understanding?

Children can be lured into holiday books at Thanksgiving time after playing a simple "gratitude" game. Starting with each letter of the alphabet, have your students think
of something they are grateful for. Each child can use one
letter, or they can each have a complete gratitude alphabet.
Tommy may be grateful for apples, arrows or his Aunt Anna;
Mary may follow by being grateful for babies, balloons and
bubble-gun. The teacher would be wise to be grateful for
each of the children in her room--Agnes, Bobby, Carla and
Chris, etc. After struggling with "Z, " the question might
be asked, "Are you more grateful for things or for people?"
And "why?" Then, "What were the Pilgrims who celebrated
the very first Thanksgiving most grateful for?" Read a book
aloud and find out together! Then add their gratitudes to
your class alphabet list. The impetus may well carry you
into another book which will have another suggested activity,
and your Thanksgiving reading will be well under way.

After a Halloween story hour one small listener picked up an armload of witch books and announced, "My hallow isn't weenie--it's gigantic!" And so are all children's appetites for books when they have been presented as fun activity-producing springboards at holiday times.

How were the titles chosen for Celebrating with Books? From the many good books available on holiday themes, a variety of familiar ones were selected for their easy availability, as well as for their diversity. Many other books would serve equally well, with similar activities to those suggested here. New ideas for projects may be triggered off in your classroom, for once a teacher starts thinking in terms of books as aids to whetting excitement in the curriculum, fresh ideas will multiply. Some titles have been chosen to serve a special purpose: easy-to-read, an example of a parody as a literary form, a sample of the folk literature of a nation, etc. The important question here is not so much "which good holiday books shall I use," but rather, "am I using the many wonderful resources available to me?"

The grade level indications given are meant as a guide, not a restriction. You will find the books which appeal most to you, and it is your love of them and appreciation of their message and the activities they stimulate which will determine how successful they are in your classroom. Some books which are obviously written for the very young are designated "all ages" because they contain something of universal value or appeal. Such a title is Something for Christmas by Palmer Brown. A truly good book can rarely be pinned down arbitrarily between two age levels! No two children are exactly alike, and no two classrooms receptive to the same stimulus at the same moment. Use your intuition, and feel free to step outside our age-level suggestions, which were never meant to limit, but only to indicate a possible starting point.

How were the holidays chosen? Generally, this book emphasizes the major holidays about which a wide variety of books are readily available. Others, such as U.N. Day, were included because material supports major areas of the curriculum. After experimenting with the holiday books and activities suggested in Celebrating with Books and witnessing the joy they generate, you may want to track down books on lesser known holidays and adapt the activities we have suggested to fit them. There are infinite ways of bringing life and light into a classroom, and holiday times give added zest to the daily routine.

The inclusion of Fall Birthdays and Spring Birthdays of favorite authors makes year-round birthday parties in your classroom a possibility. Each celebration will be adding a dimension to the appreciation of books and the people who create them. A lively correspondence may even develop if the children decide to send their favorite author a birthday card, or a letter relating how the day was celebrated in the classroom. When an author comes to life, his/her books often do the same!

An extra bonus is included with the books on Spring in the Easter section and the books on Fall in the Thanksgiving section. There is no time of the year which does not lend itself to celebration. The world and the life which inhabit it are inexhaustibly fascinating, and our classrooms should be lively and living proofs of this fact.

The last chapter includes specific examples of how a growing awareness, appreciation, and use of holiday books can vitalize the development of study skills. One little pebble of information from a shared book can drop into the pond of a child's consciousness and start the circles of search and discovery broadening out into the infinite joy of discovery and achievement. Research then becomes not only an achieved skill and a useful tool, but results in the natural exhilaration which comes from all true learning.

Unfortunately many children have had only depressing experiences with books. Never having been read to at home, they lack the motivation to impel their progress at school. Falling behind immediately, their self-image shrinks. A conviction that they are inadequate is generally accompanied by the even more vehement conviction that books are ogres. These ogres appear horrendous, insurmountable, forever lurking to gobble up their fragile egos.

Such distortions, left uncorrected, result in deprived children. For books are not only peeks out into life, but they insure our children of inner lives not stultified by stagnation. Every child deserves to be exposed to the stimulus which is uncovered when the print is peeled off the pages to reveal the ideas locked within. Released, these ideas are a natural catapult into activities. Together, they insure a life of perpetual regeneration. What a gift for all children!

A teacher who cares will take the time and the holiday opportunities to expose our future citizens anew to the

light and life bursting behind the covers of books.   When the
focus is taken beyond phonics and drills, beyond the format
of print and glue and cardboard, and the book is used rather
as a building block to climb upon for new views of the pano-
rama of life, eyes will begin to sparkle.   A book cannot be
shoved into a reluctant reader's hands and work an instant
cure.   But a book shared by an enthusiastic teacher who is
full of ideas and activities to help make it not only palatable,
but irresistible, can work miracles.   Celebrating with Books
is meant to help you work such miracles....

　　　Which is reason enough to celebrate!

COLUMBUS DAY

Background Information

October 12th is the day for celebration of the discovery of the new world by Christopher Columbus in 1492. Columbus first went to sea at the age of 15. His experience with ships led to a concurrent interest in map making and this fostered the idea that it might be possible to sail all the way around the world. With the financial aid of Queen Isabella of Spain, Columbus outfitted three ships. He set sail with a crew of 120 men and after a long and difficult voyage landed in the West Indies, not at first realizing that he had discovered a new land. Columbus Day was declared a national holiday by President Benjamin Harrison in 1892.

Titles Suggested for Use	Suggested Grade Level
Dalgliesh. The Columbus Story	K-3
D'Aulaire. Columbus	2-6
Heimann. Christopher Columbus	3-6
Judson. Admiral Christopher Columbus	2-6
Kaufman. Christopher Columbus	3-4
Norman. A Man Named Columbus	1-3

While the above titles were chosen for brief review in this section because of the wide variety of approaches to the subject that they represent, every school and public library will have many equally suitable titles which can be shared with students and used as springboards to many of the activities which are suggested following the reviews.

Dalgliesh, Alice. The Columbus Story. Illus. by Leo Politi.
  Scribner's, 1955. (K-3)
     This beautifully written, carefully researched history
is meant to be read aloud to children. Leo Politi's colorful
full-page illustrations help the reader to visualize the times
and challenges faced by this early explorer and to appreciate
more keenly his accomplishments. This outstanding author-
illustrator combination has created a book of lasting value
which should be a first choice to read aloud to primary children.

D'Aulaire, Ingri and Edgar Parin. Columbus. Illus. by
  the authors. Doubleday, 1955. (2-6)
     This team of author-illustrators has produced many
classic biographies for children which can be enjoyed through
a wide range of grade levels. The writing is accurate, detailed and colorful, presenting enough challenge for independent intermediate readers, and yet, the stunning illustrations
are appealing to younger students. The text is excellent for
reading aloud.

Heimann, Susan. Christopher Columbus. Franklin Watts,
  1973. (3-6)
     A fascinating collection of authentic prints, documents,
and maps from the time Columbus was actually alive is held
together by a carefully researched text on his life and experiences. An index adds value to the text. Children of
many ages will be lured and intrigued by the maps and original prints if the teacher sets the stage by talking about
them. Given an enthusiastic introduction to the book, older
students will want to pursue this interesting and well-written history/biography on their own.

Judson, Clara Ingram. The Picture Story and Biography of
  Admiral Christopher Columbus. Follett, 1965. (2-6)
     A ten-page picture story prefaces the longer biography
in this competent work by a notable author of juvenile biographies. The illustrations in the beginning synopsis are in
full color and could be read aloud to younger classes. The
full biography which follows includes detailed and close-up
maps of the conclusions of the four voyages and should interest older readers.

Kaufman, Mervyn. Christopher Columbus. Illus. by Nathan
  Goldstein. Garrard, 1963. (3-4)
     One of the World Explorer Series, this book is de-
signed for young readers who love adventure and exploration.

The writing is designed for third and fourth graders and is both lively and filled with dialogue and excitement. The end pages are useful in providing maps of Columbus' first voyage and in labeling many points of interest in his life. The symbol of the World Explorer books is an astrolobe, about which an eager researcher might want to delve further and share his or her findings with the class.

Norman, Gertrude. A Man Named Columbus. Illus. by
    James Caraway. G. P. Putnam's Sons, 1960. (1-3)
        An easy-to-read basic story of Columbus, his child-
hood, exploits, and eventual achievements. This could be
read aloud to pre-schoolers but is most effective as a biography independently tackled by a beginning reader who has
been motivated to know more about this courageous explorer.

Activities

        All of the foregoing books and many others found in
your school or public library will instill an appreciation and
awe of the man who achieved so much against such tremendous odds over 500 years ago. In preparation for a celebration of Columbus Day there are many activities which the
reading of these books could stimulate and which will help
children focus on the courage and accomplishments of this
remarkable explorer.

1) After seeing the many illustrations in these books, the
children will be eager to draw or paint or color or create
in clay or in wood or other three-dimensional material,
those tiny sailing vessels which surmounted the seas ... the
Nina, the Pinta and the Santa Maria. Different artists' versions from the books will help the children to be as accurate
or as imaginative as they like, since known facts about these
ships are limited.

2) By using several of these books as references, maps can
be made to decorate the walls of the classroom depicting the
different voyages of Columbus. Maps can be carefully executed on-scale or can be drawn free-hand. If time is limited,
atlases can be used or printed maps with yarn of different
colors used to designate the routes of the different voyages.

3) A challenge for older classes could be the creation of
flat maps of the known world at the time of Columbus, which
must then be altered to become round. Don't expect perfec-

tion! Today's professional map makers are still working on
the problem!

4) Experiments can be done at all age levels with an orange
(or other sphere) as illustrated in the D'Aulaire book. See
if a paper butterfly rising behind the orange would convince
the children in your room that the world is round. Columbus
must have been very perceptive! Ask the children what other
qualities he expressed.

5) Most of these books make use of lively dialogue to tell
the story. Let a group of children volunteer to recreate
scenes from the life and times of Columbus by using dialogue
from the books, or have them write their own play after reading several of the shorter versions of the Columbus story.

6) Innumerable games can be played if you are able to obtain a simple compass. If time allows, a research project
can be undertaken which teaches children to make their own
compasses. A "treasure hunt" can then be plotted and planned
by hiding a map of the West Indies, or foil-covered coins, or
whatever, at some distant point in the school or schoolyard.
Then an "Admiral" can be chosen for a small group of children who must follow directions which have been given as
compass readings across the Atlantic Ocean (playground). As
a real challenge, one group of children might hide the treasure and write out compass directions for another group of
"explorers" to find.

UNITED NATIONS DAY

While perhaps not one of the major holidays in the United States, United Nations Day (October 24) is included in Celebrating with Books as a holiday which can motivate and stimulate student activities which lead to a greater understanding and appreciation of world cultures. A study of the folk literature of other countries can lead to discussions which are of concern to the children and to mankind itself. Indeed, in their book, Children and Books, Arbuthnot and Sutherland state that, "Whether or not children are conscious of it, these stories may become sources of moral strength-- a strength which is part faith, part courage, and wholly unshakable."

The sharing of folk tales of many world cultures provides an opportunity for children to taste a tiny bit of a culture very different from their own and to stretch their minds and imaginations as they come to appreciate the beauty of a language whose structure is unfamiliar to their ears and customs which are different from their own.

While only a few titles are reviewed in this section, the possibilities for finding and using appropriate titles in almost any school library are endless. United Nations Day can serve as a stepping-off point for the study of the folk literature of other countries, or as a day which will culminate all of the activities which have taken place beforehand.

The History of the Holiday

United Nations Day is proclaimed annually by the President of the United States to commemorate the founding of the United Nations Organization on October 14, 1945. The need for a world organization to work for peace was felt by many nations following World War II and, in 1945, delegates from fifty nations met in San Francisco to set up such an organ-

ization. The goals of the United Nations are in part: "To
save succeeding generations from the scourge of war; to promote social programs and better standards of life; to practice tolerance and to live together in peace."

A number of books are available on the United Nations Organization which are appropriate for the elementary
student. One of the best of these is M. Sasek's This Is the
United Nations (Macmillan, 1968). Illustrated with large full-
color drawings, the book presents basic information about
the UN in an attractive, eye-catching and easy to understand
manner. Included is a brief history of the founding of the
United Nations, the Preamble to the Charter, the location,
the flags of all member nations (as of the date of the book),
a tour of the works of art found in the building, and illustrations and explanations of the General Assembly, The Secre-
tariat, The Security Council, The International Court of Jus-
tice, the Economic and Social Council, The Trusteeship Council and UNESCO. A more detailed explanation of this world
organization can be found in Edna Epstein's The First Book
of the United Nations (Watts), which is illustrated with actual
photographs of the United Nations buildings and operations.

Activity

Ask for volunteers to compile a list of member nations
of the United Nations. Another volunteer committee can survey daily newspapers and collect articles for the bulletin
board. A third committee can visit the school library and
collect at least one book on each member nation. The Macmillan series noted above is excellent for use. Among other
titles in this series (all by M. Sasek) are: This Is Ireland,
This Is Hong Kong, This Is Paris, This Is London, This Is
Rome, This Is Munich, This Is Greece, etc. Let each child
choose one nation to represent at a mock General Assembly
Meeting, discover some basic information about that nation,
and prepare his nation's stand on questions which might come
before the General Assembly. Current issues from the news
articles can be considered, or hypothetical questions can be
developed.

Alternate Activity

After sharing several of the cities or countries of the
world books, have the children prepare a book similar in

format about your own city. Each child can have a different landmark to illustrate. These could be chosen after a field trip or walk around town. If your class would like to have pen pals in a classroom in another country, this would motivate the preparation of such a book to send overseas.

The Study of Folk Literature

It is quite probable that no one school library will contain all the specific titles reviewed in this section. They have been selected as representative of the many themes, styles and motifs found in folk literature and as examples of the literature indigenous to the countries from which the tales come. In introducing folk tales it might be helpful to point out to students those basic elements of literature which are found in most tales.

As applied to folk literature these elements are: 1) A very brief setting of the scene; 2) Events told in the order in which they happen (no flashbacks); 3) One-dimensional characters with little explanation for the behavior of a character; 4) A clear contrast of some type; for example, "good" characters pitted against evil characters; 5) An abrupt or swift ending to the story; 6) A use of language or style of narrative indigenous to the country of origin.

Students will enjoy completing a chart similar to the one which follows as they read and enjoy a variety of tales.

Folktales will usually contain one or more of the following:	Title of the Folktale	
	A STORY, A STORY	PERRONIQUE
1. Person or object with magic or supernatural powers.	X	X
2. Animals or objects which talk.	X	
3. One or more tasks to be accomplished	X	X
4. Use of wits or trickery	X	X
5. Wishes or dreams fulfilled	X	X

6. Chain-of-events stories

7. Explanations of nature

8. Tales of legendary heroes or
   of real events

Themes found in folktales are:

1. The power of love & kindness		X
2. Good vs. evil		X
3. Happiness is preceded by pain		X
4. Use of wits can overcome force or power	X	X

Other Elements

1. Use of numbers 3 & 7	X	X
2. Magic flower always a rose		X
3. Magic fruit always an apple		X
Country of Origin	Africa	Celtic

Titles Suggested for Use	Suggested Grade Level
Frost. Legends of the United Nations	3-6
Fromm. Pumpernick and Pimpernell (Germany)	K-3
Haley. A Story, A Story (Africa)	3-6
Jameson. One for the Price of Two (Japan)	3-6
Michel-Dansac. Perronique (Celtic)	4-6
Mosel. Tikki Tikki Tembo (China)	K-4
Paterson. Waltzing Matilda (Australia)	4-6
Ransome. The Fool of the World & The Flying Ship (Russia)	3-6
Rinkoff. The Pretzel Hero (Austria)	3-6

Rockwell.   The Monkey's Whiskers (Brazil)   2-4

Rockwell.   Tuhurahura and the Whale
   (New Zealand)   all ages

Walker.   New Patches for Old (Turkey)   2-4

Watts.   While the Horses Galloped to
   London (England)   3-6

Yolen.   Greyling (Scotland)   4-6

Titles about the United Nations

Epstein.   First Book of the United Nations   4-6

Sasek.   This Is the United Nations   3-6

Frost, Frances.   Legends of the United Nations.   Illus. by
   Karl Schultheiss.   McGraw-Hill, 1943.   (3-6)
      The United Nations referred to in the title are those
nations who were Allies in World War II.   If this title is not
available, any collection of folk tales from many lands will
suffice.   The reason for the selection of this particular title
is found in the author's preface: "I have tried to present
those [stories] which seem to me most representative of the
national characteristics of each country.   Whether the tales
are romantic, fantastic, moralistic, humorous, or courageous,
all are indigenous and a part of the inheritance of children
for generation after generation, and a part of the essential integrity of the men and women into whom the children grew."
With the exception of Czechoslovakia, more than one tale is
included for each of the following countries: Great Britain,
Poland, China, Norway, Russia, Greece, India, United
States, Netherlands, Mexico, France, Yugoslavia, Brazil,
Canada, Australia and Belgium.

Activity

      What fun it would be to share a different tale (one from
each country) each day!   Beginning about three weeks before
United Nations Day, read aloud each day and discuss with the
class one story from each country.   Help children to distinguish those words, terms and customs in each story which
emphasize the national characteristics of each country.   To
help students remember the various stories, begin a chart on
the bulletin board which gives the title of each story, the
country of origin, the main characters and a one-sentence

annotation of the story. A different student can be appointed
each day to prepare this information for the story read that
day.

Several days before United Nations Day ask the children to choose their favorite character from any of the
stories which have been read and to come to school on U. N.
Day dressed as that character. When the big day arrives,
children will enjoy guessing which character each has decided to be, and small teams of these story characters can
visit other classrooms to briefly tell about the character they
have chosen to be and the story in which the character is
found. (Be prepared for a raid on the folk tale section in
the library as other eager students search for tales from
many lands!)

Fromm, Lilo. Pumpernick and Pimpernell. Illus. by the
       author. Doubleday, 1967. (K-3)
       In this colorfully illustrated German folk tale, two
gentle friends, Pumpernick and Pimpernell, live together in
a small cottage surrounded by a peaceful garden. Their days
are so quiet and uneventful that even their dog, Pudding the
Brave, does not have to worry about living up to his name.
One day the garden is invaded by a host of strange characters, including a huge blue mouse who goes to sleep on the
roof of the cottage. Pumpernick, Pimpernell and Pudding
hide in a tree and watch the ensuing battles among the in-
truders. Finally the strangers wear themselves out fighting
and go to sleep, giving the two friends and their dog a
chance to rid themselves of their unwanted guests.

Activity

Read the story aloud, up to the point where the in-
truders go to sleep. Point out to the children that when an
author creates a story, the author often has to choose from
many possibilities to bring the story to a successful ending.
Ask the children to think about the best means for getting
rid of the mouse, Pete the Drifter, and the Noise Man.
(Answers can be logical or fantastic.) Divide the class into
groups of four to six students. Let each group discuss possible endings and develop an ending which they think is best.
Groups can then share their possible solutions and all will
enjoy hearing the solution the author has chosen. (Some students may like their own endings better!)

Haley, Gail. A Story, A Story. Illus. by the author. Athe-
    neum, 1970. (3-6)
        This is an account of the origin of the African "Spider
Stories," richly told in the repetitive style of the African
storyteller. In the beginning, all stories belonged to the sky
god, so there were no stories for the children to hear.
Ananse, the Spider Man, visited the sky god to buy some of
the stories but the price was high indeed. After much resourceful effort, Ananse does manage to pay the price, which
is the leopard-of-the-terrible-teeth, the hornet-who-stings-
like-fire, and the fairy-whom-men-never-see. For his clever-
ness and bravery Ananse is rewarded by the sky god, who
declares that "all my stories shall belong to Ananse and
shall be called spider stories. "

Activity

        The author notes in the introduction the African style
of storytelling. She says, "At times, words and phrases are
repeated several times. Africans repeat words to make them
stronger. For example: 'So small, so small, so small'
means very very small. " Children might enjoy working in
small groups to prepare a familiar tale for telling in the
African style. Working together on an old tale (Little Red
Riding Hood, the Three Pigs, the Teeny Tiny Woman), all
adjectives can be examined and repeating phrases substituted
where appropriate. For example, The Teeny Tiny Woman
might become "The little woman, the little woman, the little
woman. " As stories are shared, ask students to decide
which is the more effective method of storytelling (the use of
adjectives or repeating phrases?), or does each method have
its place?

Jameson, Cynthia. One for the Price of Two. Illus. by
    Anita Lobel. Parents Magazine Press, 1972. (3-6)
        In this clever tale of trickery from Japan, an old man,
Kichei, buys a beautiful heifer and takes it to show to his
friend, the Master Clog-Maker. So much does Kichei boast
about the animal that the Clog-Maker and his apprentice decide to trick the old man by stealing the heifer as he takes
it home. They succeed, not only once but three times, each
time selling the beast back to Kichei, who does not realize
until the third time that he is buying his own animal. Finally, Kichei does catch on to the joke that is being played on
him, and bearing the tricksters no ill will, he invites them
to a meal at his house.

Activity

Note that tales of trickery are very common in all
lands. The Ananse stories from Africa are tales of animal
trickery, as are many of the Br'er Rabbit stories from the
United States. Allow volunteers to explore the folklore section of the library to locate as many tales of trickery as
they can. Children who enjoy storytelling can choose one of
the tales to prepare for telling to the class. After the tales
have been enjoyed, ask the students to look for similarities
in the tales regardless of the country of origin. Why do
they think these similarities exist? (This is a question which
has puzzled scholars to this day!)

Michel-Dansac, Monique. Perronique. Illus. by the author.
    Atheneum, 1969. (4-6)
    When the orphan, Perronique, learned of the power
held by the evil wizard, Rogear, he was determined to re-
gain from the thieving wizard the magic lance and cup stolen
from the king. To accomplish this he must overcome seven
dangerous elements to reach the wizard's castle, including a
deadly forest, a three-eyed giant, a lion with serpents for a
mane, and a lady pest of the deadly kiss. He succeeds
through bravery and the use of his wits, and restores the
objects to their rightful owner.

Activity

This Celtic tale combines all of the elements of the
classic fairy tale, the use of the numbers 3 and 7 (3 soldiers,
7 tasks), the magic fruit (an apple) and flower (a rose), the
poor but honest hero, a wicked, evil wizard, magic objects
(the lance and cup), supernatural beings and good overcom-
ing evil. List these elements on the chalkboard as children
note them. Divide the class into groups and challenge each
group to write a modern fairy tale using as many of the elements as they wish. The tales may be presented in any
method of a group's choosing: as a play, a pantomime with
narrator, a puppet show, a write-on filmstrip, a slide-tape
presentation, a roll movie, a shadow play, etc.

Mosel, Arlene. Tikki Tikki Tembo. Illus. by Blair Lent.
    Holt, Rinehart & Winston, 1968. (K-4)
    A Chinese folktale delightfully retold, about a first-
born and revered son named Tikki Tikki tembo-no sa rembo-

chari bari ruchi-pip peri pembo! Second sons in China were given hardly any names at all, and Tikki's little brother was named Chang. When Chang disobeys his mother's warning and falls into the well, it is not hard for the first-born to get help. But when he, himself, falls into the well, it takes Chang so long to say his brother's name that help is almost too late to save him. From that day to this, "the Chinese have always thought it wise to give all their children little, short names instead of great long names. "

Activity

This is another tale which lends itself easily to drama- tization. These skits can be done with little or no props, for children are masters at the art of imagining. The well, the ladder, the stream and the clothes can all be imagined. All that is needed is the four characters; their actions will enable the audience to see the imaginary props. All the children will enjoy joining in on "Tikki tikki tembo-no sa rembo-chari bari ruchi-pip peri pembo. " The sing-song may be heard on the playground for weeks to come!

Paterson, A. B. Waltzing Matilda. Illus. by Desmond Dig- by. Holt, Rinehart & Winston, 1970. (4-6)
A. B. Paterson, the Australian poet, wrote "Waltzing Matilda" in the late 1800s. The song, which is rich in the language and folklore of the country, became known all over the world. It tells the story of a swagman camped in a bill- abong, who caught a jumbuck and put it in his tucker-bag. Pursued by the police, he jumped into a water hole and drowned and his ghost sings today in the billabong the sad, sad song, "Waltzing Matilda. "

Activity

This is a made-to-order book for dramatization, com- plete with musical background! Be sure students understand the meaning of the Australian terms. A glossary in the back of the book gives clear explanations of them. Then let the whole class learn the song (easy to do with such a favorite). One part of the class can sing the story while other members act out the various parts (the swagman, the sheep, the police). Then roles can be switched so that all have a chance to sing and to act out the story.

Ransome, Arthur. The Fool of the World and the Flying
    Ship. Illus. by Uri Shulevitz. Farrar, Straus & Gi-
    roux, 1968. (3-6)
        In this classic Russian folktale, the Czar offers his
daughter in marriage to anyone who can bring him a flying
ship. In one poor hut in the land live three brothers with
their parents. The two clever brothers are given a warm
send-off by their mother as they set off to find such a ship.
The third brother is the Fool of the World and when he decides to seek the ship, his mother pays little attention to
him. Through a meeting with the Ancient the boy is told
how to secure the flying ship and once he has the ship and
sets sail, he encounters and takes aboard the ship a group
of men who have strange powers. Through the help of the
Listener, the Swift-goer, the Far-shooter, the Eater, the
Drinker, the Moujek with the straw and the Peasant with the
fagot of wood, the Fool of the World overcomes all of the
obstacles put in his way by the king and wins the hand of the
princess.

Activity

        Folktales often contain characters with magical powers.
Note that there were seven such characters taken aboard the
ship in this story, seven being a frequently used number in
folk literature. As students share tales from many countries
they may be interested in finding out more about the magic
people who are a part of the folklore of each country. Barbara Softly's Magic People Around the World (Holt, Rinehart
& Winston, 1969) is a good introduction to legendary dwarfs,
mermaids, giants, etc.
        As students learn about the world's magic people they
may enjoy creating life-sized images of these folk characters
or of the magic characters from The Fool of the World and
the Flying Ship. Large rolls of paper can be unrolled on the
floor and while one student lies on the paper, others can
trace around him or her with magic markers. Details within the figure will be determined by the particular magical
character the students want to create. Such characters, when
completed, can line the hallway of the school, and at scheduled times during the day students can take turns acting as
"tour" guides to explain the characters and their powers.

Rinkoff, Barbara. The Pretzel Hero. Illus. by Charles
    Mikolaycak. Parents Magazine Press, 1970. (3-6)
        This tale of excitement and suspense is based on an

actual event which has, over hundreds of years, become part
legend and part fact.   In 1529, Hans Wetzel served as an apprentice to Emil, "the greatest pretzel maker in all of Austria. " Hans was kept so busy in his job that he sometimes
forgot the soldiers in the streets, who were there to defend
Vienna against the invading Turks.   During a moment of rest,
Hans heard digging under the floor of the bakery.   His master sent him to raise the alarm, for sure enough, the Turks
were tunneling under the city.   With this warning the Aus-
trian soldiers were able to defeat the Turks, and a grateful
king granted the pretzel makers a special coat of arms to
hang in front of their shops.

Activity

        The last illustration in the book is of the coat of arms
which might have been adopted by the pretzel makers.   The
shield on a coat of arms identifies the owner.   In this case,
the symbols on the shield are the products of the pretzel
makers' art.   The symbol or symbols on other shields can
tell of some great event in the owner's life or of some outstanding quality he possesses.   The crest on the pretzel
maker's shield is a lion, indicating loyalty, royalty and
bravery (and in this case, that the coat of arms was award-
ed by the king for the loyalty to the crown shown by the bak-
ers).   Many coats of arms also contain a motto by which the
wearer tries to live.
        Children will be interested in finding out more about
heraldry and coats of arms and can do so using reference
books from the library.   After examining as many pictures
of coats of arms as they can find, let each child design his
own coat of arms.   He might identify his family name through
the use of initials on the shield or through the use of a symbol (for example, a child with the last name of Carver can
symbolize the name with a small drawing of a knife and
piece of wood).   Other symbols which appear on the shield
can tell of an outstanding event in the child's life or show
some quality he would like to possess.
        Before developing a motto for the shield, children
may want to examine well-known mottos in our country's history or research the motto which is contained on the seal of
their state or other states.   The motto the child chooses
should reflect his beliefs or feelings.
        The completed coats of arms should be displayed in
as prominent a place as possible (perhaps the bulletin board
in the school library?), for many children to enjoy.

Rockwell, Anne. The Monkey's Whiskers: A Brazilian Folk-
    tale. Illus. by the author. Parents Magazine Press,
    1971. (2-4)
        A curious monkey leaves the forest to visit a town;
there, he watches a barber shaving a man. The monkey
asks the barber to shave him but when the job is done, the
monkey decides he wants his whiskers back. When the barber explains that he cannot return the whiskers, the monkey
takes the barber's razor. Thus begins a series of incidents
in which the monkey gives away an object on one day and demands it back on the next. The recipients who take the
monkey's gifts as gifts rather than a loan are unable to return them and must give the monkey something else instead.
The story runs full circle when the monkey demands the barber's daughter and the barber, in turn, promises to restore
the monkey's whiskers in eight days. When this is successfully accomplished, the barber demands the return of his
razor and the monkey beats a hasty retreat back to the forest.

Activity

        Long before money was used by people, goods and
services which were felt to be of equal value were exchanged.
This was called barter. Suppose there was no money and
for one week everything that a family purchased had to be
purchased by barter. Ask each student to compile a list of
five things that he or she might want or need to purchase
within a week's time. Opposite each item listed, list the
goods or services that the student might exchange for the
item. Let students compare lists to see if they agree or
disagree on the value of the goods or services they exchange
for the things they want to buy.

Rockwell, Anne. Tuhurahura and the Whale. Illus. by the
    author. Parents Magazine Press, 1971. (all ages)
        A young New Zealand island boy angers the wicked
sorcerer, Kiki, when he cuts down a tree near Kiki's home
to build a canoe. Kiki changes himself into the form of a
boy and begs to go fishing with Tuhurahura. Through trickery, Kiki leaves Tuhurahura in the sea and paddles for home,
only to be caught in "the whirlpool that lies at the end of
the world." Tuhurahura is rescued by Tutunai, the whale,
and brought safely home. The author has used photographs
of the Maori Tribe of New Zealand, taken about 1880, as the
basis for the details of clothing, artifacts and architecture
used in the illustrations.

Activity (1)

In the story it states that: "Tutunai taught Tuhura-hura a song. He told him it was the song whales sing when they are happy." Perhaps one or more students in the class would enjoy composing the words and a simple melody for such a song. The class can learn the new song and sing it with or without accompaniment.

Activity (2)

Older children who enjoy this story will enjoy hearing the Newbery Award Recording of Call It Courage (Miller-Brody Prod.). This is the story of an island boy, Mafatu, who also becomes adrift in the sea. The vivid illustrations of ocean life in both books can lead to an interest in finding out more about ocean life. A class effort to produce an "ABC of Ocean Life" book for the "rare book shelf" of the school library can result in each child doing research on one ocean creature and adding his page to the book when it is written and illustrated.

Walker, Barbara and Uysal, Ahmet. New Patches for Old.
    Illus. by Harold Berson. Parents Magazine Press, 1974.
    (2-4)
This is a hilarious Turkish tale of Hasan, the shoe-maker, who buys holiday gifts for his family and new trous-ers for himself. However, the trousers are much too long and need to be shortened by a width of three fingers; but neither his wife, nor his mother or daughter has time to un-dertake the task. Hasan shortens the trousers himself, only to find on the next day that each of the women of his family has secretly shortened them as well. The only answer to the problem is to add patches to secure the right length, thus exchanging new patches for old.

Activity

Discuss with students those terms or customs which are characteristic of Turkey (holidays beginning in the even-ing with prayers for the dead, measurements, the illustra-tions of the unique architecture and clothing of the land).

Borrow, if possible, two folk tales for each child in your room (from school or public library). Give each child two books explaining that you will play a game called "New Books for Old." At a given signal each child passes on one

of the two books (keeping the one which most appeals to him).
As the new title is received, each child again makes a decision as to which title he will keep. After 8 or 10 passes
each student should have chosen one title which really appeals
to him and which can be read and shared with the class
through oral summaries.

Watts, Mabel. While the Horses Galloped to London. Illus.
   by Mercer Mayer. Parents Magazine Press, 1973.
   (3-6)
         Beautifully illustrated with authentic details of an ear-
lier England, this is the story of a group of travelers who
more than fill a coach headed for London. Sherman, who is
taking a stew pot to his grandmother, has orders to guard it
with his life! The pot is so large that soon the other passengers begin to complain. Sherman tries holding the pot on
his lap, putting it in an overhead rack, placing it on the floor,
and finally giving up his seat to the pot while he stands for
the rest of the trip. None of these solutions satisfies the
passengers until Rough Roger, the highwayman, appears to
rob the coach. Sherman's quick mind helps him to use the
pot to save the day, all "while the horses galloped to London!"

Activity

         In addition to the authentic illustrations, many English
expressions are found in the story. Examples are highwayman, cockles, mussels and the names of various English
coins--shillings, farthings, sovereigns, guineas and silver
crowns. Children may not be aware that in traveling to other countries, it is necessary to exchange American money
for the currency of each country. Begin a chart on the bulletin board to which all of the children can contribute. Head
the chart with the words: "If I Traveled to." List countries
of the children's choosing down one side of the chart. (A
new country might be added each time a folktale from that
country is read.) The chart can be similar to the one below.

If I Traveled to	The money I would need is called
Argentina	Peso
Burma	Kyat

Denmark   Krone

Great Britain   Pound

    One or more students may want to volunteer to find
the exchange rates for the currency mentioned in While the
Horses Galloped to London.   (A television set would cost
how many sovereigns? A candy bar would cost how many
farthings? etc.) Completing the chart will prove to be an
especially good research project for those students who always seem to complete other assignments ahead of most of
the class.

Yolen, Jane. Greyling. Illus. by William Stobbs. Collins-
    World, 1968.   (4-6)
    A wistful and beautifully told tale of the Shetland Is-
lands, based on the ancient legends of selchies, seals who
take on human forms. A fisherman and his wife long to have
a child. When the fisherman finds an orphaned baby seal on
the beach, he wraps it up in his shirt to take to his wife.
Upon removing the wrapping she finds a strange and lovely
child, whom they name Greyling. He grows to young man-
hood, never having been allowed to touch the sea. The fisherman is caught in a treacherous storm. None of the towns-
people dares to attempt to rescue him. Greyling plunges
from a cliff into the sea and saves his foster father, but the
contact with the water turns him into his original form. The
seal heads joyously back out to the sea.

Activity

    Have the class learn the song at the end of the book,
"The Grey Selchie of Sule Skerrie." The class could then
divide in half, with some of the children singing the song and
the others swimming as seals in the waves. The children
might enjoy making seal masks which they could slip on as
they slide into the imaginary sea, and slip off as they emerge
back on to the classroom beach.

HALLOWEEN

Background Information

The celebration of Halloween dates back to the ancient Romans, who honored their dead on a special day during the year. Most of the Halloween customs, however, come to us from ancient England, where very powerful priests called Druids sacrificed animals to the Gods in the fall of each year. On All Hallows Eve fires were built and men with pitchforks stood guard to keep away evil spirits which they believed returned to earth on this one night of the year. The Druids believed that cats were sacred and housed the spirits of the dead. Other symbols of Halloween date back to these ancient times as well--the pumpkin, the haystack and the witch, which was a symbol of the evil spirits which were believed to fly about on this one night of the year.

Titles Suggested for Use		Suggested Grade Level
Adams.	A Woggle of Witches	K-2
Balian.	The Humbug Witch	K-3
Battles.	The Terrible Trick or Treat	1-4
Bright.	Georgie and the Noisy Ghost	K-2
"	Georgie to the Rescue	K-2
"	Georgie's Halloween	K-2
"	Georgie and the Robbers	K-2
Coombs.	Dorrie and the Blue Witch	K-2
DeLage.	The Farmer and the Witch	K-2
"	The Old Witch & the Wizard	K-2
"	What Does a Witch Need?	K-2

20

Devlin.	Old Black Witch	K-3
Haley.	Jack Jouett's Ride	3-6
Hopkins.	Hey-How for Halloween	all ages
Kent.	The Wizard of Wallaby Wallow	all ages
Lexau.	Millicent's Ghost	1-3
Mariana.	Miss Flora McFlimsey's Halloween	K-3
Martin.	A Ghost Story	all ages
Sendak.	Where the Wild Things Are	K-2
Slobodkin.	Trick or Treat	K-3
Thayer.	What's a Ghost Going to Do?	K-2
Viorst.	My Mama Says There Aren't Any Zombies ...	all ages
Wahl.	Cristobol and the Witch	3-6
Wilkins.	The Pumpkin Giant	3-6
Zemach.	Duffy and the Devil	all ages

Also Included

A Ghostly Circle (game)	3-6
Witch or Ghost (game)	3-6

Adams, Adrienne. A Woggle of Witches. Illus. by the author. Charles Scribner's Sons, 1971. (K-2)
    Take a wild ride with a woggle of witches on Halloween night! Fortified with bat stew, off they go to twist, turn and glide through the sky. From the moon they descend to the Earth, where they are startled by a parade of costumed children. Exhausted from their wild ride, the witches finally return to their home in the woods and a late supper of "bat stew and spiderweb bread."

Activity

    Children will enjoy making their own witches to "fly" around the classroom. Draw a pattern on a ditto master similar to the one pictured here. Each child receives a dittoed sheet which contains both the broom and witch patterns. Materials children will need include: crayons, scissors, paste, string, toothpicks.

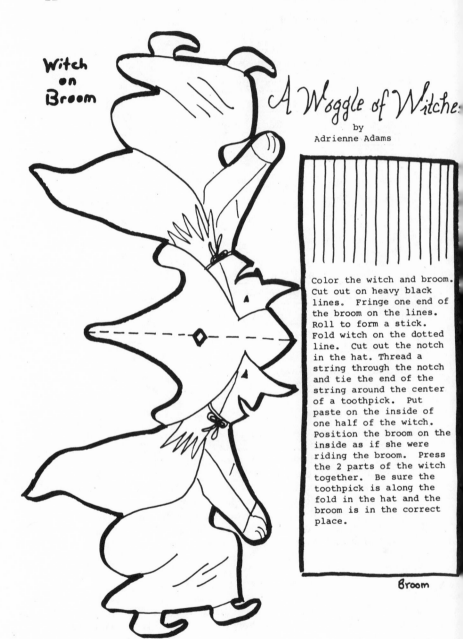

Witch on Broom

A Woggle of Witches

by
Adrienne Adams

Color the witch and broom.
Cut out on heavy black
lines. Fringe one end of
the broom on the lines.
Roll to form a stick.
Fold witch on the dotted
line. Cut out the notch
in the hat. Thread a
string through the notch
and tie the end of the
string around the center
of a toothpick. Put
paste on the inside of
one half of the witch.
Position the broom on the
inside as if she were
riding the broom. Press
the 2 parts of the witch
together. Be sure the
toothpick is along the
fold in the hat and the
broom is in the correct
place.

Broom

Instructions:

1) Color the broom and cut it out.
2) Fringe one end of the broom on the lines.
3) Paste the wrong side (uncolored side) of the broom handle and roll the paper to form a stick.
4) Color and cut out the witch.
5) Fold on the dotted line.
6) Tie the end of the string around the center of the toothpick.
7) Cut out the notch in the hat and thread the string through the notch.
8) Put paste on the inside of one half of the witch and position the broom on the inside as if she were riding the broom.
9) Press the two parts of the witch together; be sure the toothpick is along the fold in the hat and the broom is in the correct place.

Ideas for Use:

1. Mobiles--Hang in the windows or from the ceiling.

2. Bulletin board--Make a yellow moon on a dark background. The witch is patterned after the witch on the page of the book that simply says, "Whee...." The bulletin board could be arranged like that scene, or perhaps with the next two pages in mind, which would provide a lighter background. The strings could be eliminated on the witches that are attached to the board, but a few witches hanging to flutter in the fall breeze would be most eyecatching.

3. Mural--The children may want to paint tall trees on newsprint or butcher paper. The witches could be hung in place to tell the story. This would be an attractive display for the hallway of your school.

Balian, Lorna. The Humbug Witch. Illus. by the author. Abingdon Press, 1965. (K-3)
     This little book bursts with life as little witch, disappointed that her magic does not work, gradually takes off her funny black shoes, her plaid apron, her handknit black wool shawl, her slightly squashed tall black pointed hat, her orange gloves, her long stringy red hair, and finally ... her mask! Then the little girl exposed underneath goes to bed.

Activity

         This is a delightful story to share using a flannel
board.   All the accouterments can be scotch-taped over the
large simple drawing of a little girl, and can be removed at
the appropriate time in the story.   A small group of children could help to make the drawings of the various items
of disguise and thus be in on the surprise when the little girl
is unmasked at the end.   This story is also fun to tell with
a child performing all the action and disrobing.   This is a
delightful Halloween tale for the youngest, because it gives
a comfortable assurance that underneath all the scary masks
are smiling children.   A primary class might enjoy prepar-
ing it as a story hour to share with a kindergarten.

Battles, Edith.   The Terrible Trick or Treat.   Illus. by
      Tom Funk.   Young-Scott Books, 1970.   (1-4)
         Christopher decides to collect the best treats by going
out "trick or treating" earlier than his friends.   But to his
surprise, all he manages to collect are some vitamin pills,
a piece of someone's mind, chicken pox, a dog bite, a tooth
brush and some good advice.   The good advice tells Christo-

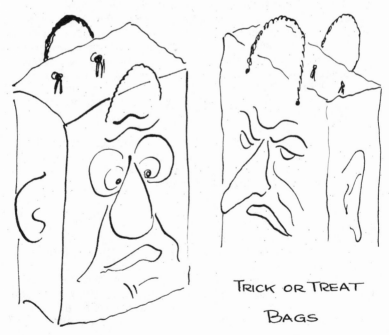

TRICK OR TREAT

BAGS

pher that he might do better if he did his trick or treating
on the right day! It seems that without realizing it he went
not only early in the evening, but a whole day early!

Activity

Trick or treat bags! Ask each student to bring to
school two large grocery bags which fit inside each other.
Put a little glue on the bottom of the inner bag before slip-
ping it inside the other. Attach string-crochet handles
through both bags and decorate the outside of the bag with
cut paper noses, eyes and ears, and crayons or felt-tip marker drawings (see illustration).

Bright, Robert. Georgie and the Noisy Ghost. Illus. by
    the author. Doubleday, 1971. (K-2)
        When Mr. and Mrs. Whittaker rent a beach house for
the holidays, Georgie, the ghost, Herman, the cat, and Miss
Oliver, the owl, move in, too. However, they soon discover
that the old house has its own very noisy ghost! It is the
ghost of Captain Hooper who continued to howl nightly because
in all his life he had never received a medal. With Georgie's
help, the Captain has a chance finally to win a medal (and
thus cease his howling) when he saves Mr. and Mrs. Whittaker who are lost in a fog at sea.

Bright, Robert. Georgie to the Rescue. Illus. by the au-
    thor. Doubleday, 1956.
        The Whittakers take a trip to the city along with Her-
man, Georgie and Miss Oliver. Herman does find a mouse
to chase in the hotel and Georgie finds a squeaky elevator,
but trouble arises when Miss Oliver, the owl, tries to find
a place to sleep during the day. She chooses the city flag-
pole. She is soon captured and taken to the zoo, and
Georgie and Herman undertake the job of rescuing her.

Activity

These and other Georgie stories by Robert Bright will
prove especially appealing to primary children. To develop
the idea of story sequence, separate sets of "Ghost Cards"
can be made for each Georgie book. Six cards for each
book should be made, each listing an event from the story.
After the story has been read to the class or the child has
read the story to himself, he can get the appropriate set of
cards for the book and try putting them in order of the events

as they happen in the story.   Events listed for Georgie and
the Noisy Ghost might be: 1) Mr. & Mrs. Whittaker leave
for the summer cottage; 2) They all see the cottage for the
first time; 3) The tired Whittakers go to bed for the night;
4) The ghost of Captain Hooper appears; 5) Mr. and Mrs.
Whittaker go out in their boat and get lost at sea; 6) Captain
Hooper saves the Whittakers and gets a medal.

    Other delightful Georgie stories and events for which
sequence cards can be made are:

Georgie's Halloween (Doubleday, 1958)

1) Georgie hides on Halloween night; 2) The Whittakers go to
the village; 3) Georgie arrives at the party; 4) Georgie is
seen by the children; 5) Georgie runs home; 6) Georgie
blows out the pumpkin.

Georgie and the Robbers (Doubleday, 1962)

1) Mr. and Mrs. Whittaker leave for church; 2) The robbers
arrive; 3) The robbers steal the furniture; 4) Georgie fright-
ens the robbers; 5) The neighbors return the furniture;
6) Georgie tells his tale to the mice.

Coombs, Patricia.   Dorrie and the Blue Witch.   Illus. by
    the author.   Lothrop, Lee & Shepard, 1964.   (K-2)
    When Big Witch leaves the house, Dorrie invites a
strange blue witch in for tea.   It is obvious that she has
made a mistake, so she and Gink, the cat, put some shrink-
ing powder into the refreshments that are served.   The Blue
Witch shrinks and Dorrie captures the infuriated little creature in a small bottle with a tight lid.   When Big Witch
comes home she discovers that the cook had been turned into
a cup of sugar and that Dorrie has saved the day.

Activity

    Obviously the characters in this story are GOOD
witches (with the exception of the wicked Blue Witch).   After
sharing the story with the class, ask the children if they
would like to join the witches' band which Dorrie and Big
Witch belong to.   A classroom of witches the week before
Halloween could be an exciting thing.   To add to the excitement, place a bottle with a tight lid in one corner of the
room where all "evil witches" can be imprisoned, and on

Halloween they can be magically banished. Any evil thought
or undesirable action in the classroom can be attributed to
imaginary wicked witches, who are caught and placed in the
bottle. The children will have no trouble imagining a bottle
full of shrunken evil witches, so let your imagination cavort
with the classroom full of good witches.   Bottle up bad behavior! (A slogan for the week?)

Delage, Ida.   The Farmer and the Witch.   Illus. by Gil
      Miret.   Garrard, 1966.   (K-2)
      When a farmer meets a witch strange things begin to
happen.   The cow stands on its head, the chickens lay polka-
dotted eggs and a pumpkin pie flies out the window.   The
more spells the witch decides to brew, the worse things get,
until the farmer's wife consults her book of magic spells!

Delage, Ida.   The Old Witch and the Wizard.   Illus. by
      Mimi Korach.   Garrard, 1974.   (K-2)
      A wizard tries to trade his cat for the old witch's
recipe for Halloween brew, but she refuses to trade.   When
the witch's cat presents her with three kittens she first tries
to give them away, but with no luck.   She then paints them
a different color, hoping that someone will think they are
good luck kittens, but the wizard's cat licks them clean.
Finally old witch decides to keep the kittens, not out of the
goodness of her heart, but because she discovers that they
have magical powers which will help to make her Halloween
brew the best ever.

Delage, Ida.   What Does a Witch Need?   Illus. by Ted
      Schroeder.   Garrard, 1971.   (K-2)
      Can a dog take the place of a witch's departed cat?
A witch discovers that a dog won't do at all.   Dogs can't
make fires burn, nor do they sit too well on a broomstick.
But when it comes to saving a toadstool patch from robbers,
the witch discovers that a dog is exactly what she needs!

Activity

      Ida Delage has written a number of easy to read books
with a clever witch as the heroine.   Using any of the titles
given here or any other titles in the series, discuss with the
children the characteristics of a witch.   What is a witch supposed to look like?   Where does she live?   Does she have
any pets?   How does she travel?   What does she stir around
in the large pot or cauldron she is so often pictured with?

The following game, Bat Stew, is a fun way for children to
review vocabulary words. The "ingredients" may be changed
for different groups of children, or variations may be used
to make the game suitable for many areas of study.

Bat Stew

Preparation:

1) Stew pot: outline a large stew pot on black paper. Cut
   the pot out and attach it to the side of a box. (If you
   have an old iron kettle, by all means use it!)

2) Make small patterns for bats, pumpkins, ghosts or other
   Halloween objects. Let the children cut the figures out.
   Depending on the game you are going to play, write the
   words, letters, numbers or math problems on these cut-
   out figures, which are now the stew ingredients. Put a
   staple in the top of each.

3) Broom: tie a string on the end of a toy broom handle
   and tie a magnet to the other end of the string. (A
   large spoon or soup ladle may be used to scoop out the
   brew instead of using the broom and magnet.)

Procedure: The players take turns stirring the brew and
fishing into the pot for a bat to catch on the magnet. The
player must correctly identify the word on the figure to be
able to keep it. If he/she is wrong the bat must go back
into the stew. The child with the most figures at the end
of the game is the winner.

Variations:

1) Number or letter recognition: Write a letter or number
   on each bat. Play the same as above.

2) Math games: Write one math problem on each bat. The
   child must be able to solve the problem correctly to
   keep the bat.

3) Sentence structure: Write one word on each bat, using
   words that could be used in the construction of many different sentences. The players take turns fishing for bats
   and correctly identifying the words on each. The first
   player who can make a complete sentence with his words

Bat stew ingredients

Bats --- grey
Owls ---- brown
Ghosts --- white
Pumpkins --- Orange

is the winner.   The teacher may designate the sentence length
before the game begins.

Devlin, Wende and Harry.   <u>Old Black Witch</u>.   Illus. by Har-
      ry Devlin.   Parents Magazine Press, 1966.   (K-3)
      If you were a witch and a small boy and his mother
bought your house to turn it into a tearoom what would you
do?   At first, Old Black Witch tries scaring the occupants
away.   When that fails she gets in the way of their cleaning
and remodeling and makes a general nuisance of herself.
Finally, she joins Nicky and his mother in helping to make
a success of the tearoom, and changes her evil ways entirely when she stops a robbery by turning the two robbers into
toads!

Activity

      A Halloween Bulletin Board: Let students design
their own bulletin boards.   What could be more fun than a
board filled with students' interpretations of Halloween figures

on an appropriate background!   Some media which are very
adaptive are sponge backgrounds.   Choose a solid color paper
and using a small sponge dipped lightly in tempera, paint an
appropriate color.   Dab the background until the effect is
achieved.   Cut a stencil to block out part of the background
such as trees for a Halloween theme.   An unusual effect can
be achieved with olive-green tempera (made by mixing yellow and black).   Keep moving the tree stencil to a different
location until you have a forest.   Add olive-green cut paper
witches who fly and jump from tree to tree.   Draw in the
witch figures with green chalk.   One group of students may
want to add the "Haunted Tea Room" as an inviting place for
visitors to stop!

Haley, Gail E.   <u>Jack Jouett's Ride</u>.   Illus. by the author.
      Viking Press, 1973.   (3-6)

It was not ghosts or goblins that froze Jack Jouett's
blood as he heard horses approach in the moonlight, but
"Bloody Tarleton" and his troop of British horsemen, whose
mission was to capture the leaders of the American Revolu-
tion. This is the story of Jack Jouett's exciting ride to
warn the leaders of the impending British attack.

Activity

        This true story lends itself well to research projects
for the middle grade student. Ask the class if anyone knows
whether or not Halloween was celebrated by the early American Colonists. If no one is sure, suggest that a committee
go to the library to find books on the colonists and on Halloween, to see if and how the holiday took place 200 years ago.
As the students discover that Halloween was celebrated in the
Colonies, ask each student to choose a favorite colonial figure (Patrick Henry, Benjamin Franklin, Thomas Jefferson)
and to write a fictionalized account of how the colonial hero
they chose might have celebrated Halloween as a child.

Hopkins, Lee Bennett. Hey-How for Halloween. Illus. by
    Janet McCaffery. Harcourt Brace, 1971. (all ages)
        What better way to enjoy Halloween than through a
sampling of poetry chosen especially for that holiday! Lee
Hopkins has developed this spine-tingling collection of poems
by choosing from the finest of poets. While, as the book
suggests, you may not all be able to share these poems "in
a candle-lit room at Midnight with a black cat at your side,"
it might be possible to draw the shades and turn off the
classroom lights on a cloudy afternoon and read to children
by candlelight.

Activity

        Poetry sharing sessions in the school library are popu-
lar during holiday times. Students should be notified well in
advance of the time and date of a scheduled poetry sharing
session. Students who wish to share should sign up with the
librarian, including the name of the poem each plans to share.
Poems can only be shared if they are memorized. No special length is required. Both those who share and those
who come to listen will profit greatly from the experience if
one requirement is that students choose only poems they especially like. As an added attraction, students may want to
make appropriate color-lift slides to be projected as each
shares his or her poem.

Kent, Jack.   The Wizard of Wallaby Wallow.   Illus. by the
     author.   Parents Magazine Press, 1971.   (all ages)
     The Wizard of Wallaby Wallow has so many spells
that he has a time getting and keeping them organized.   His
spells can turn people into almost anything.   One day as the
wizard is busily engaged in trying to guess the contents of
bottles with missing labels, a mouse knocks on his door and
pleads for a spell.   As the mouse contemplates what kind of
a spell can be in the bottle he receives, he undergoes a
change in his thinking and decides that being a mouse is not
so bad after all.

Activity--Primary

     Primary children might have a special browsing time
in the school library to see how many books they can find
for their classroom reading table on witches and wizards.
During the browsing time encourage the children to choose
one book about imaginary people (witches and wizards) and
one about real people.   Stress the idea that books can tell
about both real and imaginary things.

Activity--Intermediate

     Class members might look through old Time Maga-
zines or other weekly or daily news sources to find some
particular "ill" in the world or in a community that needs
to be cured.   Each student should create a spell designed to
cure the ill he has found.   The student should give both the
ingredients and procedure for using the spell, as well as its
intended effect.

Lexau, Joan.   Millicent's Ghost.   Illus. by Ben Shecter.
     Dial Press, 1962.   (1-3)
     Just before Millicent leaves for a visit to Aunt Aga-
tha's house, her brother, Charles, warns her that the house
is haunted.   Millicent explores the big old house and, with
Charlie's warning on her mind, she has one fright after another.   A dress form is mistaken for a headless woman.
She decides that a cat's eyes belong to a witch and that
Great Aunt Agatha in her nightgown is surely a ghost.   As
Millicent's fears are explained away, she finds that when
they were small visitors to Aunt Agatha's, her brothers were
even more afraid of seeing ghosts than she was.

Activity

This story introduces the power of suggestion as a motivating force. Students might want to demonstrate this idea further by playing a "Power of Suggestion" game. Ask each student to bring to school a box which contains an item of his or her choosing. Each box should be labeled with a suggestion as to what it MIGHT contain. (For example: a dried, shriveled apple might be labeled "a shrunken head.") Some labels should be honest and others not. Number each box and place on a table or along the windowsill. As students who are blindfolded reach into each box and feel each object they should later record in their notebooks, by number, what they think the object is. The student who identifies the most objects correctly wins the game.

Mariana. Miss Flora McFlimsey's Halloween. Illus. by the author. Lothrop, Lee & Shepard, 1972. (K-3)
    A favorite doll-house character, Miss Flora McFlimsey, takes off on the back of a witch's broomstock with Pookoo, the cat, but she wiggles and falls off. Little Oscar Owlet tells her that the doll house is being vandalized by five goblins. Tiny Timothy Mouse hides in the folds of her cloak and has many brave suggestions. Another ride on the back of Oliver Owl takes them to the Witches' Ball, where they tell Pookoo of the troubles. He comes to the rescue and they arrive home in time to hear midnight strike, when all goblins, ghosts and witches vanish into the night.

Activity

Children will enjoy setting the song of the witches to music.

Mumblety, jumblety, tippledetay
Rumplety, rumplety, ripplederay

They will also enjoy making paper-bag masks of the variety of characters in the story. Since as many witches, goblins, spooks and animals can be at the witches' ball as there are children in the class, everyone can be included and encouraged to choose his or her own character. The paper bags should fit over the children's heads and have eyes cut in the right spots for peeking out. Then start the music for a witches' ball! It is helpful to remember (if it gets too lively) that at the stroke of 12 they must all vanish until next All Hallow's Eve.

Martin, Bill, Jr. A Ghost Story. Illus. by Eric Carle.
     Holt, Rinehart & Winston, 1970. (all ages)
        Pictures and text blend in perfect harmony in this lit-
tle book, which takes the reader step by step to dark and
scary places. When an evil spirit escapes from a bottle it
retraces the steps and settles in the pocket of the little boy.
The story ends (as all good ghost stories should) with the
words, "He's got you!"

Activity

        This small book is a good example of how a few words
can build a mood and tell a story at the same time. The
story might be read to the class at Halloween time, with students instructed to close their eyes and picture in their
minds the scenes in the story. After they have used their
own imaginations let the children see Eric Carle's depiction
of an evil spirit. Ask, "Is there any one way to picture
such a spirit?" Ask the children to draw their own interpretations of the spirit coming from the bottle. When these
are completed and displayed, ask each child to be prepared
to answer the following questions about his spirit: Does it
have a name? Where did it come from? What makes it
evil? How can the evil spirit be overcome?

Sendak, Maurice. Where the Wild Things Are. Illus. by
     the author. Harper & Row, 1963. (K-2)
        A small boy named Max is sent to bed without supper.
With no one to talk to, he soon lets his imagination run wild
and his bedroom is transformed into a mystical jungle filled
with "wild things." Max becomes King of the wild things,
each one wilder than the last, and they all do his bidding no
matter how fearsome they may appear. Max finally decides
to return to real life and the end of the book finds the little
boy back in his bedroom where supper is waiting for him.

Activity

        This book can be enjoyed as a Weston Woods 16mm
film as well. For information concerning Weston Woods
films and filmstrips write to Weston Woods, Weston, Conn.
06880. After sharing the book or the film with children,
talk with the children about the possibility of dramatizing the
story for others to enjoy. Each child can create his own
wild thing mask using paper bags and scraps of yarn, string,
colored construction paper etc. Stress that these wild things

do not have to resemble those in the book but should be each
child's own creation. A reading of the text along with appropriate background music (for example, Saint-Saëns' Danse
Macabre) and pantomimed action by students wearing their
original masks can make a delightful Halloween program for
other classes to see. As each child creates his own mask,
have him tell about the creature he plans to be: is it a shy
or bold creature? Does it walk, hop, crawl? Encourage
children to show how their creatures will act.

Slobodkin, Louis. Trick or Treat. Illus. by the author.
    Macmillan, 1959. (K-3)
        The children who lived on Willow Street went "trick or
treating" every Halloween. Since they went only to homes on
Willow Street and were expected at every home, there were
always treats to be had and no tricks. One Halloween, however, the children saw a light on in an old house that had
previously been vacant. A ring of the bell brought a little
old man to the door who immediately told his visitors that
he had no treats so he would have to do tricks for them.
And tricks he did! They were such amazing feats that the
children forgot all about visiting other houses as they watched
Mr. Purple do one trick after another. As he explained to
the parents who came looking for their children, he was a
former professional magician and since he and his wife had
just moved in that day, there was no time to have treats
ready for the children so he did tricks instead! From that
Halloween on, Professor Purple provided the tricks while the
other parents provided the treats and a grand Halloween celebration was had by all.

Activity

        Students might well enjoy putting into practice the new
meaning given to the old expression "Trick or Treat" in this
story. Suggest that it might be fun to offer to do a "trick"
for the neighbors that children visit, and that students explore the section in the school library which contains books
on magic tricks. Those who learn new tricks might enjoy
demonstrating them for the class before trying them out on
Halloween night.

Thayer, Jane. What's a Ghost Going to Do? Illus. by Sey-
    mour Fleishman. William Morrow & Company, 1966.
    (K-2)

Poor Gus, the friendly ghost, lost his home when it was sold to be torn down. He moved in with another ghost who didn't like his banging and clanking. He moved in with a mouse but the conditions were too crowded. So he returned to his condemned home and was able to convince the buyers to make it into an historical museum, complete with ghost!

Activity

To have a classroom full of friendly ghosts at Halloween, have each child make a ghostly face on a white paper bag, stuffed and tied at the bottom. These can be attached to the ceiling at different heights and create a ghostly, but quiet atmosphere. This story might prompt a visit to an historical museum if there is one in your community, where the children can appreciate the things Gus loves (and try to catch a glimpse of him?).

Viorst, Judith. My Mama Says There Aren't Any Zombies, Ghosts, Vampires, Creatures, Demons, Monsters, Fiends, Goblins, or Things. Illus. by Kay Chorao. Atheneum, 1973. (all ages)

A small child wonders if he can believe his mother when sometimes she makes mistakes. She told him his wiggly tooth would fall out on Thursday and then it stayed until after lunch on Sunday. She still gets lost on the way to Christopher's house. So how can she be SURE that there isn't a goblin in the dresser drawer? But, after all, sometimes mothers are right.

Activity--Primary

Students would enjoy drawing something which THEY have pictured in their closets or under their beds at night. Ask them if they were ever right. Talk about the fun of imagining things as long as one knows they are not true. Teachers can share an experience where they made a mistake or imagined something which was not so.

Activity--Intermediate

This is a perfect title to use in a game of "Book Title Charades." Divide the class into two teams. Each team decides on several book titles to be pantomimed. A title is given to a member of the opposite team and they are timed as they try to guess it from the antics of their team-

mate who is acting it out.   If the title is guessed correctly
within the alloted time the team receives five points.   That
team in turn gives a title to a member of the opposing team
to act out.

Wahl, Jan.   Cristóbol and the Witch.   Illus. by Janet Mc-
    Caffery.   G. P. Putnam's Sons, 1971.   (3-6)
        Cristóbol is enticed by a witch to help her get back
her treasures from her three wicked sisters.   The boy
agrees to help, knowing that his reward will be the burro
that he desires above all else.   The task, however, proves
difficult and requires the help of a flycatcher, an owl and a
fox.   When the treasures are finally regained they turn out
to be just what a witch would covet--"squeaking rats, neck-
laces made of porcupine quills, and 100 shoes for the left
foot only," among many other things.   The witch does keep
her promise and Cristóbol's friends accompany him home to
help explain his new acquisition, the burro.

Activity

        Ask each child to search at home for some unwanted
or discarded object that a witch might treasure.   Remind
children that dangerous items (knives, pins) should not be
brought to school.   As each child shows his or her object to
the class there should be an explanation as to why a witch
might want the object and what the witch will do with the object.   Some children might use their explanation as the starting point for a written story.   Objects can be displayed on a
table with captions or stories written by the students.

Wilkins, Mary E.   The Pumpkin Giant (retold by Ellin
    Greene).   Illus. by Trina Schart Hyman.   Lothrop, Lee
    & Shepard, 1970.   (3-6)
        Many years ago there lived a fierce pumpkin giant in
a castle surrounded by a moat filled with bones.   The plump-
er the children, especially little boys, the tastier for the
giant his meals would be.   Everyone feared this monster and
even though the king promised to knight anyone who could cut
off its head, no one was brave enough to make the attempt.
Finally, a simple farmer, Patroculus, in attempting to save
his roly-poly son, Aeneas, threw a potato into the pumpkin
giant's mouth and he choked.   When Patroculus cut off the
giant's head, the seeds scattered and the resulting pumpkin
patch attracted Aeneas.   He soon discovered the tastiness of

the pumpkins and convinced his mother to try cooking one.
Thus the pumpkin pie was born.   The king rewarded the
peasant family and Aeneas married the Princess Ariadne
Diana.   Every year thereafter he carved a giant head for
her.

Activity

Who can carve the fiercest pumpkin face? If the supply of pumpkins is limited, who can draw the most fearsome
one?   When the class votes a winner it can be traced onto
a real pumpkin.   After it has been carved and properly appreciated the children can cut it into small pieces, boil them
and make their own delicious pumpkin pie.   (A small portable oven might be brought from home.) Keep the classroom
door closed if you don't want the rest of the school peaking
in to see where the irresistible fragrance is coming from!

Zemach, Harve and Margot.   Duffy and the Devil.   Illus. by
    the author.   Farrar, Straus & Giroux, 1973.   (all ages)
When Squire Lovel's housekeeper, Old Jane, can no
longer spin, sew or knit, the squire hires a serving girl
named Duffy to take over these chores.   Duffy accepts the
job to escape her former bad-tempered employer, but alas,
she has none of the skills needed for making the Squire new
clothes.   In her distress Duffy strikes a bargain with the
Devil, one which she soon comes to regret.   While the good
Squire does finally manage to save Duffy from her own folly,
he does so by losing all of his clothes in the process.

Activity--Primary

Students can compare this story with the old tale,
Rumplestiltskin, noting similarities and differences.   Bring
out the fact that many of the old tales are told just a little
differently in different parts of the world.   Ask the school
librarian to send to the classroom a number of easy-to-read
folktales and fairytales.   Encourage the children to read the
stories and to recall if they have heard other stories which
are similar in some way to those read.   It is also fun to
compare more than one version of the same story as told or
illustrated by different authors and artists.

Activity--Intermediate

This story is rich in "made up" words which often

serve better than real words in describing a person or event. Examples are: "bufflehead," "gashly," and "squinny-eyed." Other fun words created by the Zemachs are "whillygogs," "whizamagees," "confloption" and "fuggy-home." Ask students to give some thought to creating their own new descriptive words. Along with the "made-up" word, the student must give a definition. For example: "floothing" might mean walking slowly through a mist or fog.

After words are created and defined they can be illustrated by their creator for inclusion in a "New Words Dictionary." Illustrations can be mounted on 8 1/2 x 11 cardboard or laminated and bound into book form. Such a book might be donated to the school library for its "Rare Book" shelf (a shelf set aside for books written by students which are truly "one of a kind" or rare books).

A GHOSTLY CIRCLE

The names of two favorite ghosts are hidden in the circle below. Move around the circle beginning with the starred letter and reading every other letter to find the names of the ghosts. Fill in the blanks in the book titles with the name of the correct ghost.

1) _____ and the Magician   _____ and Wendy

2) _____ and the Noisy Ghost   _____ and Wendy's Adventure

3) _____ and the Robbers   _____ in Ghostland

4) _____ Goes West   _____ and the Friendly
                                                  Ghost

5) _____ to the Rescue   Published by
6) _____'s Christmas Carol   Harvey Comics

       by Robert Bright

WITCH OR GHOST (A Card Catalog Game)

Directions:

       Check the card catalog in your school or public li-
brary to see how many of the book titles below you can complete. If a title appeals to you, try to locate the book in the
library and borrow it to read. If you enjoy the book, tell
your classmates about it. (* indicates a book for older
readers.)

1. Benchley, Nathaniel. _____ Named Fred. (Harper,
    1968)

2. Snyder, Zilpha. _____ of Worm. (Atheneum, 1972)*

3. Brenner, Anita. The Timid _____. (Young-Scott,
    1966)

4. Bright, Robert. Georgie and the Noisy _____.
    (Doubleday, 1971)

5. Speare, Elizabeth. The _____ of Blackbird Pond.
    (Houghton-Mifflin, 1958)*

6. Gage, Wilson. The _____ of Five Owl Farm.
    (World, 1966)*

7. Byfield, Barbara. The Haunted _____. (Doubleday,
    1973)

8. Estes, Eleanor. The _____ Family. (Harcourt
    Brace, 1960)*

9. Garfield, Leon. Mr. Corbett's _____. (Pantheon,
    1968)*

10. Carmer, Carl. The Screaming _____. (Knopf,
    1956)*

11. Bennett, Anna. Little _____. (Lippincott, 1953)

12. Burch, Robert. The Jolly _____. (Dutton, 1975)

13. Fleischman, Sid. The _____ on Saturday Night. (Little-Brown, 1974)*

14. Place, Marian. The Resident _____. (Washburn, 1970)*

15. Raskin, Ellen. _____ in a Four Room Apartment. (Atheneum, 1969)

16. Stephens, Mary Jo. _____ of the Cumberlands. (Houghton-Mifflin, 1974)*

17. MacKellar, William. _____ Around the House. (Dodd, 1974)*

18. Coombs, Patricia. Dorrie and the Blue _____. (Lothrop, 1964)

19. Yolen, Jane. The _____ Who Wasn't. (Macmillan, 1974)

20. Peck, Richard. The _____ Belonged to Me. (Viking, 1975)*

Note to the teacher

The sample titles given here will give you a good idea of the many books written for children with the words witch or ghost in the title. Your school library should have ample suitable titles for you to use in making up a quiz similar to this one. Your quiz will be more successful if it is done chiefly for primary grades or chiefly for intermediate grades (rather than starring books for older readers). Many first and second grade students are able to use the card catalog in schools where regular library instruction is a part of the program. Grades three through six should have no problem with the quiz and some very difficult titles might be starred.

Answers to Witch or Ghost Quiz

1 ghost; 2 witches; 3 ghost; 4 ghost; 5 witch; 6 ghost; 7 ghost; 8 witch; 9 ghost; 10 ghost; 11 witch; 12 witch; 13 ghost; 14 witch; 15 ghost; 16 witch; 17 ghost; 18 witch; 19 witch; 20 ghost.

THANKSGIVING (FALL)

Background Information

Many ancient people held harvest festivals. That of the early Romans was in honor of the god, Ceres. The Greeks honored their goddess of agriculture, Demeter. Hundreds of years ago harvest feasts were held in England. Thus, Thanksgiving as it is celebrated in the United States is based on these old world customs which the English settlers brought to the new land. The Pilgrims who came to these shores in 1620 faced many hardships that first winter, but by the following harvest time, with the help of the Indians, a bountiful harvest was forthcoming. The first Thanksgiving was a three-day feast to which the Pilgrims invited over 90 Indians.

Abraham Lincoln declared Thanksgiving a national holiday in 1863 and traditionally it is a day when families get together for a feast, fellowship, church services and football games.

Titles Suggested for Use	Suggested Grade Level
Balian. Sometimes Its Turkey Sometimes Its Feathers	K-2
Bartlett. Thanksgiving Day	2-4
Burch. The Hunting Trip	all ages
Carrick. A Clearing in the Forest	all ages
Dalgliesh. The Thanksgiving Story	2-4
Devlin. Cranberry Thanksgiving	all ages
Hays. Pilgrim Thanksgiving	all ages
Kahl. The Duchess Bakes a Cake	K-2

Kumin. Follow the Fall   K-2

Miles. A Day of Autumn   K-6

Parish. Granny and the Indians   K-3

Spier. The Fox Went Out on a Chilly
        Night   all ages

Tresselt. Autumn Harvest   all ages

Titles Suggested for Use	Suggested Grade Level
Van Woerkom. The Queen Who Couldn't Bake Gingerbread	2-4
Wyndham. Thanksgiving	3-6
Zion. The Meanest Squirrel I Ever Met	K-2
Zion. The Sugar Mouse Cake	K-2

Additional Activity

Fall Birthdays	all ages

Balian, Lorna. Sometimes Its Turkey, Sometimes Its Feathers. Illus. by the author. Abingdon Press, 1973. (K-2)
    One day Mrs. Gumm found a freckled egg. She was so excited that she told her friend the cat that she planned to hatch the egg and have the turkey for Thanksgiving dinner. Sure enough, the egg did hatch and the hungry turkey ate everything in sight--even the cat food. But Mrs. Gumm didn't mind, for she saw the turkey getting fatter and fatter and thought of the nice plump turkey that she would have by the time Thanksgiving arrived. When Thanksgiving Day finally arrived Mrs. Gumm DID have the turkey for dinner, but as a guest rather than as a main course.

Activity

    Children will enjoy planning a menu for a Thanksgiving dinner which does not include turkey. Ask students to suggest what favorite foods might be included in a Thanksgiving dinner. List their choices on the chalkboard. Kindergarten children and new first graders can vote on the choices which have been listed and perhaps illustrate their favorite food for display on a "Favorite Thanksgiving Dinner" bulletin board. Second graders will enjoy making their choices from all of the foods listed and designing their own menus for display.

Bartlett, Robert M. Thanksgiving Day. Illus. by W. T. Mars. Thomas Y. Crowell, 1965. (2-4)
    An easy-to-read account of the harvest festival from

the early Romans to today, this book might serve as a springboard to first research activities for second and third grade students and an informational source for fourth grade remedial students. The major part of the book deals with the Pilgrim Thanksgiving. A simple, but accurate account of the holiday.

Activity

Duplicate the Thanksgiving word puzzle given here. All information needed to solve the puzzle can be found in Thanksgiving Day. Challenge students who successfully complete the puzzle to choose another Thanksgiving word (turkey, pumpkin, etc.) and make up their own word puzzle based on information from the book for others to solve.

1. They came to Plymouth in 1620.
2. The voyage took _____ days.
3. Thanksgiving was a feast of _____.
4. The Pilgrims were _____ to God.
5. Governor of the Plymouth Colony.
6. They helped the Pilgrims.
7. An Indian chief.
8. The Indian who helped the Pilgrims most.

(1) P - - - - - - -
(2) - I - - - - - -
(3) - - L - - - - - - - -
(4) G - - - - - - -
(5) - R - - - - - -
(6) I - - - - - -
(7) M - - - - - - - -
(8) S - - - - - -

Burch, Robert. The Hunting Trip. Illus. by Suzanne Suba. Scribner's, 1971. (all ages)

A hunter and his young wife start off into the wilds to shoot something for their dinner. From the tiny grass finches to mourning doves, squirrels, ducks, a wild turkey and, finally, a deer, the hunter is stopped from shooting by the wife, who always has an excuse to make her husband wait for something better. The husband finally trades his bullets at the crossroads store for peanut butter and cherry jam, which they eat with the eggs, milk and biscuits that the wife prepares for dinner. Thinking over the events of the day the wife remarks, "Oh, husband, what fun it is to go hunting!"

Activity--Primary

Ask the children why they think the young wife kept
suggesting other animals to her husband when he was about
to shoot.   Ask them why she thought it was fun to go hunting.
Mention the term, vegetarian, and ask if anyone knows someone who is a vegetarian.   Let the children work together to
prepare a Thanksgiving menu which would not include a turkey
or other meat and yet would have a satisfactory amount of
protein.

Activity--Intermediate

If children are not familiar with the term "satire,"
discuss this term with them.   Ask in what way Robert Burch
has created a satire, and what his purpose was in doing so.
Some children whose parents like to hunt may indicate that
the killing of wild life is not always a bad thing.   Visits to
the classroom by representatives of both views (hunters vs.
those who oppose the killing of wildlife) should stimulate
thought and research on this question.   Research can include
a class letter to the Conservation Commission of your state,
to obtain information on game laws and the reason for them.

Carrick, Carol and Donald.   A Clearing in the Forest.   Illus.
    by the authors.   Dial, 1970.   (all ages)
    A man and his boy build a home in the forest and en-
dure the winter hardships which follow.   Mice eat holes in
the cupboards, and rains wash away the planted seeds; yet,
they stay and care for the wild creatures around them.   When
spring arrives, the forest repays the man and boy for their
care of its creatures and the two receive gifts from nature
in abundance.

Activity--Primary

Ask the children to recall the many things that the
forest gave to the man and the boy.   Make a list of these
things on the chalkboard and encourage children to add to the
list other good things we receive from nature.   Children
may want to write their own "nature dictionaries," using
definitions and illustrations of things we receive from nature.

Activity--Intermediate

This is a good book to use at Thanksgiving to start

children thinking about the many gifts from nature on which
we are dependent and our responsibility for conserving our
natural wildlife and improving our environment.   Letters
might be written to your state's conservation bureau request-
ing information on the wild areas remaining in your state and
on good conservation practices.

Dalgliesh, Alice.   The Thanksgiving Story.   Illus. by Helen
     Sewell.   Scribner's, 1954.   (2-4)
          This is the story of the Pilgrims told from the view-
point of one family, the Hopkins, from the time they left
England on the Mayflower until the first Thanksgiving.   The
hardships of the ocean crossing and their fear of the new
land, Indians and death are accurately told but not over-
emphasized.   Courage and triumph are the message and the
reader will be grateful, too, at that first feast!

Activity

          The diagram of the Mayflower and the map of Cape
Cod and Plymouth may inspire children to make their own
Mayflowers by cutting out sails and fastening them to the
chips they have drawn.   For older children, research on
ocean voyages of this same period will be exciting.   Students
can discover what food was taken on a voyage, what the hold
contained, how long a voyage might last, and the dangers involved.   Maps of the United States, Massachusetts and Cape
Cod, each pin-pointing Plymouth, can be made as research
activities progress.

Devlin, Wende and Harry.   Cranberry Thanksgiving.   Illus.
     by Harry Devlin.   Parents Magazine Press, 1971.   (all
     ages
          Prejudice is the theme of this thoughtful but fun story.
Grandmother has long distrusted Mr. Whiskers, the old sea
captain whom Maggie, her granddaughter, liked very much.
Her famous recipe for cranberry bread was a secret which
many had tried to learn, and she was convinced that Mr.
Whiskers was after it.   She especially hated his scraggly
beard which she thought dirty and unkempt.
          On Thanksgiving Day Grandmother and Maggie always
invited one guest each, someone alone or poor, to share dinner with them.   This year Grandmother chose a dapper
gentleman from town who was alone, and Maggie, to her
Grandmother's dismay, chose Mr. Whiskers.   There was a

sharp contrast between the two men, Mr. Horace dressed
like a dandy, carried a cane, brought a gift and smelled of
lavender. Mr. Whiskers smelled of clams and seaweed,
dressed as usual and was all but hidden by this tremendous
bush of a beard. Grandmother was not very cordial to the
Captain but with the delicious meal, and Maggie's trying hard
to be gracious to everyone, the occasion went well until Maggie and Grandmother cleared the table and went into the
kitchen. Grandmother warned Maggie to keep an eye on Mr.
Whiskers and, as Maggie peeked through the door, she saw
Mr. Horace find the secret recipe. Mr. Whiskers chased
him and retrieved it. Of course, Grandmother now saw him
in a new light; she looked past the beard to the man behind
it.

Activity--Primary

Stress the idea with younger children that it is not
always wise to judge by appearances. Explain the idea by
using Grandmother and Mr. Whiskers as examples. Tell
them that there is a word for this kind of behavior--preju-
dice. Start a bulletin board or flannel board. Through the
year let the children bring in pictures that they have found
of people, places or things that look funny to them. Each
time you put a picture on the board, put a one-, two-, or
three-word caption under it stating some positive quality that
might be attributed to the person, place or thing. For example, a picture of a very fat person might be captioned
"loving," or "makes good cookies." Switch the captions
around often so that there will be no definite associations.
It can also be a source of humor as you rearrange captions.
Imagine a tough looking workman with the caption, "Makes
good cookies."

Captions under places or things will probably need to
be, as a rule, more accurate than hypothetical, and more
stationary than mobile. A picture of an operating room in a
hospital with surgeons and nurses in masks would bear the
caption in simple terms for young minds, "Make us well."
A picture of an abstract painting would have the caption,
"Pretty colors."

Activity--Intermediate

Let older children conduct a survey. Give each one
a question to ask. Instruct them to write the question at the
top of a page and number each response, collecting twenty
answers over a period of one week. They are allowed to

ask anyone but not to record the names of those asked.
Questions are along these lines: What do you think of men
who wear very long beards? What do you think of ladies
with bleached hair? What do you think of people with freck-
les? When the data are collected have the children write the
answer most frequently given, the number of times given, the
second most frequent answer and number of times, and their
conclusion. Is prejudice evident in your survey?

Hays, Wilma Pitchford. Pilgrim Thanksgiving. Illus. by
    Leonard Weisgard. Coward-McCann, 1955. (all ages)
    This is an account of the first Thanksgiving Day as
celebrated by the Pilgrims and the Indians and told through
the eyes of real children who were there. Damaris, her
brother Giles and Little Dog all have different reactions to
the celebration. This book accurately begins where Alice
Dalgliesh leaves off in The Thanksgiving Story. The fears
of Damaris will be understood as she faces the unknown ele-
ment of the Indians. But fear is soon replaced by understanding and friendship.

Activities

    A mock Thanksgiving day can be held, with the chil-
dren choosing whether they want to be Pilgrims or Indians.
Simple costumes can be created from paper by the children.
Paper feathers can designate the Indians and paper hats or
bonnets for the Pilgrims. If there is time to do more,
girls will enjoy long skirts and aprons and boys can turn
their pants legs into breeches with the use of large rubber
bands or by stuffing their pants legs into their socks. Sam-
ples of one or more of the foods which were eaten on that
day can be made in the classroom and served. Corn meal
porridge or pudding, clam stew, berry cake or simply popcorn are possibilities.
    One fifth grade class participated in a real re-crea-
tion of the first Thanksgiving in a city park. The only foods
permitted were those which the Pilgrims and Indians had
available. It was a challenging research project! Dancing
by the Indians and marching drills by the Pilgrims wound up
the celebration. This project can be as simple or as elabo-
rate as time permits. However, research takes on a more
exciting meaning when the children know they are going to
utilize it.

Kahl, Virginia. The Duchess Bakes a Cake. Illus. by the
    author. Charles Scribner's Sons, 1955. (K-2)
      This is a delightfully funny story about a Duchess who
was the mother of thirteen children and yet found herself
one day with nothing to do. She decides therefore to bake a
cake. She sends the royal cooks away and proceeds to stir
up a batter which contains almost everything she can find in
the kitchen. When the cake begins to bake, it rises higher
and higher and higher (since she has added six times the
amount of yeast needed), and even though the Duchess tries
sitting on it, the cake continues to rise until the poor lady
finds herself up in the clouds. Neither the Duke, nor the
King nor the soldiers can figure a way to get her down, until one hungry child solves the problem. The whole kingdom
decides to "eat the Duchess down," and so they do! After
this adventure, the Duchess decides that her baking days are
over.

Activity

      If possible, reproduce on a ditto master illustrations
similar to those pictured here. The first picture of the 13
daughters can serve as the basis for a fun math lesson on
ordinal numbers. In addition, with very young children it
can serve as a lesson in color identification and in following
directions. While many types of directions can be given,
these might serve as a starting point:

    1.   Color the hat on the third little girl in row 1 green.
    2.   Color the hats red on all the girls in the second row.
    3.   Color the dress blue on the second girl in the third
       row.
    4.   Color the dresses yellow on all the girls in the first
       row.
    5.   Color the dress of the fourth girl in the second row
       orange.

The second illustration shown here gives four major scenes
from the story. Children should be directed to color the
pictures using only those colors found in the book (red, and
green). Then instruct the children to cut the pictures apart
and paste on another sheet of paper in the order in which
they appeared in the story. Children who have difficulty with
this sequencing activity should be encouraged to go back to
the book and study the pictures.

The Duchess Bakes a Cake by Virginia Kahl

Dress the children by coloring them according to your teacher's directions.

Row 1

Row 2

Row 3

Directions:
1. Color the hat on the third little girl in row 1 green.

2. Color the hats red on all the girls in the second row.

3. Color the dress blue on the second girl in the third row.
4. Color the dresses yellow on all the girls in the first row.
5. Color the dress of the fourth girl in the second row orange.

Color the pictures using only those colors found in the book.
Cut the pictures apart and paste on another sheet of paper
in the order in which they appeared in the story.

Kumin, Maxine. Follow the Fall. Illus. by Artur Marokvia.
    G. P. Putnam's Sons, 1961. (K-2)
        Told in easy-to-read verse, this is the story of a
class which has been challenged by the teacher to find signs
of fall which can be brought to school and displayed in the
classroom. Anne is disturbed because the boys in the class
seem to find more things and know more about the things
that they find than she does. After missing several good
chances to find a "fall sign" that no one else has found, Anne
finally discovers and brings to class one sign of fall that no
boy could possibly think of!

Activity

        As a delightful introduction to the fall season and
Thanksgiving, this book should encourage children to look for
signs of fall which are mentioned in the text, as well as other signs which are not. As the children find leaves, acorns,
etc. and bring them to display in the classroom, they should
be encouraged to identify and label each item. Perhaps some
members of the class will want to count all of the fall signs
mentioned in Follow the Fall and challenge themselves to find
as many or more.

Miles, Betty. A Day of Autumn. Illus. by Marjorie Auer-
    bach. Alfred A. Knopf, 1967. (K-6)
        Betty Miles has interpreted signs of fall through the
creation of vivid sensory images. The text generates a feeling of excitement as the reader hears "the wind blowing,"
sees "a V of blackbirds," feels "the quick chill," smells
"floor wax and apples," and tastes "the sweet apple juice."
This is an excellent book to use in helping children to experience the golden moments of fall through the use of all
five senses.

Activity--Primary

        Give each child a dittoed sheet of paper which has
been ruled off into five sections. Each section should be
labeled in the upper left-hand corner with the words sight,
hearing, taste, touch and smell. The heading at the top of
the sheet should read _____'s Signs of Fall. Each
child should write his or her name in the blank space. Ask
the children to draw or write the name of a fall sign they
might have seen, heard, felt, tasted or smelled in the appropriate section. If some sections are not completed, tell the

children to find signs for these sections as they travel to and from school or when they reach home. Ask them to be prepared to complete the paper the next day.

Activity--Intermediate

Use this book as an example of an author's ability to create vivid pictures or scenes through the use of sensory images. It may be necessary to define the term "sensory images" for students as those objects, scenes or situations which are brought to mind through the use of one or more of the five senses.

Ask each child to close his or her eyes and to picture a familiar room. Ask how the room might be described to someone else using as many sensory images as possible. Have children write their descriptions and read them aloud to the class. See if others can guess the room being described.

Optional

Upper grade students who enjoy reading might want to bring examples of the way in which their favorite authors create scenes through the use of sensory images. Berniece Rabe's Rass and William Armstrong's Sounder are both excellent examples of books which abound with vivid scenes which touch all the senses.

Parish, Peggy. Granny and the Indians. Illus. by Brinton Turkle. Macmillan, 1969. (K-3)
Fearless Granny Guntry pays no head to warnings about Indians as she shoos away bears and traps her own food to cook in her forest home. The Indians, however, resent Granny's intrusion into their forest home and when Granny's house burns to the ground they are relieved, thinking that Granny will go back to the town to live. Granny, however, decides to move in with the Indians. The tribe promptly deserts the camp to build Granny a new house. When she offers to come and cook for them, she is told that they will bring her all the food she needs and the only repayment needed for their "kindness" is that Granny promise to stay out of their woods!

Activity

Picture making (or drawing) is one way of helping

students to express their feelings and firm their ideas about
a story. Sometimes it is difficult to get students to fill the
page or to keep working on a picture long enough to produce
a really good picture. Have students do their drawing on
BOTH sides of the paper. Send them to the window to trace
through the picture from the back to the front. Where figures overlap, stop the lines. This will help to fill the page
and will show how some objects can appear to be in front of
other objects. Fill in the areas with color. A color wash
made with very thin tempera or water color applied over a
crayon drawing is a good addition. In applying this technique
to illustrations for Granny and the Indians, suggest that the
children draw Granny and the Indians on one side of the paper
and their Indian camp on the other. Go to the window with
the Indian encampment side up and there will be Granny in
the middle of things! Trace through all lines needed, color
the areas and add a pale brown wash. When the finished
work is displayed, ask the children to decide on the sequence
of the pictures to properly show the problem that the Indians
had with Granny.

Spier, Peter. The Fox Went Out on a Chilly Night. Illus.
    by the author. Doubleday, 1961. (all ages)
    This beautifully illustrated version of an old folk song
tells the story of a clever fox who feeds his family by stealing a goose and a duck right from under the farmer's nose.
Authentic details of a New England town and countryside are
painstakingly illustrated and words to the song are included
at the end of the book. Children will enjoy poring over the
pictures to see how many of the objects pictured they can
name!

Activity

        Students will certainly want to learn the song and sing
it along with others. Either piano or guitar accompaniment
can be used or a sing along can be done with a recorded version of the song. One recorded version appears on the Newbery Award Recording of Miracles on Maple Hill, a dramatized story which will be enjoyed by older students.
        After the song has been learned, students can take
turns dramatizing the action as the story is sung by the rest
of the class. One student can be the fox, another the goose,
another the farmer, etc. In fact, by increasing the number
of barnyard creatures there should be a part for every child.
This will make a delightful presentation to share with others
as part of a fall program.

Tresselt, Alvin. <u>Autumn Harvest.</u>   Illus. by Roger Duvoisin.   Lothrop, Lee & Shepard, 1969.   (all ages)
      Filled with the rich sights and sounds of autumn, this
book takes the reader on a nature walk which begins at the
summer's end and ends with the preparation for a Thanksgiving feast.   Numerous signs of the coming of autumn are
revealed through both text and pictures, including the feeling
of the frost in the air and the winging of flocks of birds
overhead on their way south for the winter.   Autumn is
shown as a busy time for both people and animals as they
prepare for the cold winter that is soon to come.

Activity

      This book can be shared with children of any age, so
rich is it in the images of autumn.   As the text is read
aloud, ask the children to count the number of autumn signs
that are mentioned.   If possible, take the class on an "autumn walk."   Even in the city, some signs of autumn should
be evident if the school is located in a climate where autumn
is a distinct season of the year.   During the walk children
should note as many autumn signs as they can.   After returning to the classroom students' findings can be listed on the
chalkboard.   Compare the class findings with those noted in
<u>Autumn Harvest</u> (a re-reading of the book would be helpful).
Were some of the signs similar?   Were some different?
Why, for example, would one not see flocks of birds flying
south in all parts of the United States?

Van Woerkom, Dorothy.   <u>The Queen Who Couldn't Bake Gin-</u>
   <u>gerbread.</u>   Illus. by Paul Galdone.   Knopf, 1975.   (2-4)
      An adaptation of a German folk tale with a delightful
twist.   King Pilaf of Mulligatawny could not find a bride who
could bake gingerbread the way he liked it.   He finally settled on not-too-pretty Calliope because she was wise.   She
had always wanted a husband who could play the slide trombone, but settled on King Pilaf for his kindness.   But after
the wedding they quarrelled, each disappointed in the other's
lack of ability.   The happy reconciliation comes when the
king learns to bake his own gingerbread, and the queen
learns to play the slide trombone.

Activity

      As a pre-Thanksgiving activity have the boys in your
class bake gingerbread to serve to the girls.   If no cooking

equipment is available in your school, bring from home, or
borrow, a portable electric oven.   While the boys are involved in the baking project have the girls make noisemakers
for the boys.   The simplest to do might be paper cups with
rice or beans or pebbles sealed inside for "shakers."   Each
girl could add her own decorative touches with feathers,
paint, beads or colored paper scraps.   The handles can be
decorated popsicle sticks.   These can be party favors when
the class sits to enjoy the boys' cooking.

Wyndham, Lee.   Thanksgiving.   Illus. by Hazel Hoecker.
 Garrard, 1963.   (3-6)
  A simple retelling of the Thanksgiving story including
descriptions of the early Greek and Roman harvest feasts and
the harvest celebrations in England, China and Holland.   The
section on the Pilgrims includes personal anecdotes which
make this brave band of settlers come alive for the reader.
Children will sympathize with young Frances Billington, who
must have been punished severely for almost blowing up the
Mayflower by shooting off a firecracker near some powder
kegs.   Readers may be surprised, too, to discover that
Miles Standish was so short that he was nicknamed "Captain
Shrimp."   These and other incidents concerning the Pilgrims
and their struggle to survive in the new world make for interesting reading.

Activity

  Pages 24-40 provide excellent narration for a dramatized account of the arrival of the Pilgrims at Plymouth
through the hard first winter, the meeting with the Indians
and the celebration of the first Thanksgiving.   There are
ample parts for everyone in the class.   While most of the
action can be pantomimed as a narrator reads from the text,
there may be points where students will want to work in their
own impromptu dialogue--for example, the scene where
Frances Billington thinks he has discovered the Pacific Ocean,
or the first meeting of the Indian Samoset with the Pilgrim
leaders.   Costumes are not necessary and props can be of
the simplest kind (for example, chairs to represent the Mayflower, etc.).

Zion, Gene.   The Meanest Squirrel I Ever Met.   Illus. by
 Margaret Bloy Graham.   Charles Scribner's Sons, 1962.
 (K-2)

Nibble was a small squirrel who liked to play with nuts. On Thanksgiving Day he was playing with the nuts which were to be the family's Thanksgiving dinner when a stranger, Mr. M. O. Squirrel, appeared and tricked the little squirrel out of them. Later in the day when Nibble and his family go to the Squirrel Cafe for dinner, who should be the proprietor but Mr. M. O. Squirrel. When Nibble discovers the missing nuts in the cafe kitchen he thinks of many ways to get them back until he finally hits on just the right solution to his problem.

Activity

Puppets on a Straw: Puppets often help children to verbalize and to express themselves. The two puppets on straws shown in the illustration should help the children recreate the scene in the story where Nibble goes to talk to Mr. M. O. Squirrel. Let the children make up their own conversations between the squirrels.

Materials Needed: crayons, scissors, straws, tape

Procedure: 1) Color the picture of the oak tree where the squirrel cafe is located. 2) Cut slits on the two dotted lines. 3) Color Nibble and Mr. M. O. Squirrel and cut them out. 4) Tape each squirrel to the end of a straw. 5) Insert the straws in the slits. The squirrels can move up and down during the scenes the children create. Nibble can climb up the tree and sit on the branch.

MAKE YOUR
OWN PUPPET
SHOW!

Mr. M.O. Squirrel

Color Nibble and Mr. M. O. Squirrel. Cut them out on the heavy black lines. Tape each Squirrel to the end of a straw.

Nibble

The Meanest Squirrel I Ever Met
by Gene Zion

Color the picture.   Cut slits on the two dotted lines.   Insert
the straw with M. O. Squirrel in the slit below the door of
the cafe.   Insert the straw with Nibble below the tree.

Zion, Gene. <u>The Sugar Mouse Cake</u>. Illus. by Margaret
    Bloy Graham.   Charles Scribner's Sons, 1964.   (K-2)
    When the King announced a royal pastry contest,
"Tom, the ninth assistant to the Chief Pastry Cook" decided
to enter.   His sugar mouse cake was, indeed, a work of
art.   However, when the Queen sugar mouse breaks just before the judging, and Tom's friend Tina, the mouse, takes
the Queen's place on the cake, disaster threatens.   Children
will enjoy this rollicking story filled with surprises and will
rejoice with Tom and Tina as they finally overcome seeming-
ly insurmountable problems.

Activity

Invite a baker or cake decorator to visit your classroom to tell the children about his or her art.   If it can be
arranged with the school cafeteria staff, the speaker might
demonstrate the art of cake decorating using the cakes the
children baked the day before.   (Even one or two small
cakes can be mixed and baked right in the classroom if a
small portable oven can be borrowed for a day.)   The cakes
might be given as gifts to those in the school to whom the
class might want to say thank you--the custodian, the school
nurse, etc.

FALL BIRTHDAYS

What fun to have a birthday party for a favorite author !   The party could be held in one classroom or one
class might invite another class to share in the festivities.
The list below of fall birthdays is only a beginning.   Students
can check birth dates of favorite authors in the Gale Research
Series, <u>Something About the Authors</u> or in <u>Junior Authors</u>
and <u>More Junior Authors</u>.   Whichever author is chosen for a
particular month, the invitations can be designed in the shape
of a book using appropriate titles by the author throughout
the invitation.

Example

You are invited to meet JOSEFINA
FEBRUARY and SAM BANGS AND MOON-

SHINE at a birthday party in honor
of their CREATOR, EVALINE NESS.
Don't bring A GIFT FOR SULA SULA,
just bring yourself and make A
DOUBLE DISCOVERY ... that no two of
the author's books are EXACTLY ALIKE
and that they all are fun to read!

(Book titles are in caps here but might
not be in the invitation so that children can have fun seeing how many
they can find.)

Date_____ Place _____ Time _____

Party Activities:

1.   Decorations: Illustrations and/or dioramas based on the
author's books can be used to decorate the classroom.   Mobiles of favorite characters from the author's books might
hang from the ceiling.   Papier-maché figures make attractive and permanent displays or small figures can be made
and given as favors to visiting classmates.

2.   Games: Book Title Charades are always fun with opposing teams trying to guess titles by the author given to them
by the opposite team.

Guess Who I Am?   Members of the host class can prepare
in advance short skits or scenes from the author's books or
short speeches by one character from a book for other students to guess.

What's My Line?   One student assumes the role of a book
character.   Panel members from the visiting classroom ask
questions concerning the type of work the character does.
The student assuming the role of the character can answer
only yes or no to the questions.   If a questioner receives a
no answer, the questioning passes on to the next panel member.   A time limit can be set by the teacher for the panel
to guess the type of work the character does and, if possible,
the name of the character.

Book Title Stories.   Several days before the party, list (or
have students find) all possible titles of books by the author
to be honored.   Either working with the class as a whole or

with small groups, help the children to develop stories which
use as many of the book titles in the story as possible.
Book titles should not be capitalized or underlined. The
stories can be placed on a ditto master and duplicated for
all of the students who will try their hands at finding the hidden book titles. One sample story follows:

Hidden Titles of Books by Marie Hall Ets

One day as Mr. Penny was walking in
the forest he heard my dog, Rinty barking.
Oley the sea monster was loose and has chased
Rinty up a tree. "Beasts and nonsense!" ex-
claimed Mr. Penny. "I will get my little old
automobile and chase that monster away."
"Ride me instead," said Mr. Penny's
race horse.
Mr. Penny approached the monster.
"Go away," he ordered. "You can play with me
another day. Since it is only nine days to
Christmas why don't you plan to attend the
cow's party. They are more your size. The
only other guests will be just me and Mr.
T. W. Anthony Woo. But right now, leave
my dog, Rinty alone!"
The monster went back to the sea mum-
bling "bad boy, good boy," and Mr. Penny
went back to his hobby of making automobiles
for mice.

3. Writing to the author: If the author is living, the class
can write to the author in care of the publisher several
weeks before the party, telling the author about the planned
celebration. Most children's authors are very gracious
about replying to children's letters and what a thrill it is to
read a letter from the author to the class on the day of the
party!

A partial list of children's authors with fall birthdays.

October

Ed Emberley 10/19/31
Steven Kellogg 10/26/41
Natalie Carlson 10/3/06
Edward Ardizzone 10/16/1900

Julia Cunningham 10/4/16
Phyllis Fenner 10/24/99
Louise Fitzhugh 10/5/28
Lois Lenski 10/14/93

November

Sonia Bleeker 11/28/09   Madeleine L'Engle 11/29/18
Armstrong Sperry 11/7/97   Sterling North 11/4/06
Jean Fritz 11/16/15   Kate Seredy 11/10/99
Doris Gates 11/26/01

December

William O. Steele 12/22/17   Eloise McGraw 12/9/15

CHRISTMAS

Background Information

Christmas is celebrated throughout the Christian world as the birthday of Jesus Christ. The Bible tells the story of the Christ Child who was born in a manger in Bethlehem and of the shepherds and wise men who followed a star which led them to the manger to see the newborn Christ. However, the birthday of Christ is not actually known and for 200 years after Christ's birth no celebration was held. Christians did begin the celebration after 200 A.D. and usually chose December 25, January 6 or March 25 as the date. These dates corresponded with the early pagan celebrations held by the Romans in honor of the god, Saturn, and by the sun worshippers who celebrated the coming of the winter solstice on December 21. In order to replace these pagan celebrations, Bishop Liberius of Rome in 354 A.D. set the official church celebration of the Birth of Christ on December 25.

Titles Suggested for Use	Suggested Grade Level
Alden. The Christmas Tree Forest	2-4
Bailey. Miss Hickory	2-4
Bolognese. A New Day	3-6
Briggs. Father Christmas	4-6
Brown. The Little Fir Tree	K-2
Brown. Santa Mouse	K-2
Brown. Something for Christmas	all ages
Caudill. A Certain Small Shepherd	all ages
Chafetz. The Legend of Befana	2-4
Chaneles. Santa Makes a Change	K-2
Duvoisin. Petunia's Christmas	K-2

Ets. Nine Days to Christmas	3-6
Francoise. Noel for Jeanne Marie	K-2
Hader. Reindeer Trail	3-6
Haywood. A Christmas Fantasy	all ages
Hoban. The Mole Family's Christmas	1-3
Hopkins. Sing Hey for Christmas Day!	all ages
Hurd. Christmas Eve	all ages
Hutchins. The Silver Christmas Tree	K-3
Kahl. Plum Pudding for Christmas	K-2
Keats. The Little Drummer Boy	all ages
Kent. Twelve Days of Christmas	all ages
Kingman. The Magic Christmas Tree	2-4
Lindgren. The Tomten	all ages
McGinley. How Mrs. Santa Claus Saved Christmas	K-3
Mendoza. A Wart Snake in a Fig Tree	4-6
Miller. Mousekin's Christmas Eve	K-3
Moeri. Star Mother's Youngest Child	3-6
Szekeres. A Christmas Party	K-2
Thayer. Gus Was a Christmas Ghost	K-2
Wiberg. Christmas at the Tomten's Farm	3-6

Additional Activities

Christmas Through the Eyes of Laura Ingalls Wilder	all ages
Bulletin Board Quiz	all ages
Christmas Tree Quiz	3-6
Christmas in Other Lands	4-6
A Christmas Feast	2-4
Missing Christmas Animals	3-6

Alden, Raymond. The Christmas Tree Forest. Illus. by
     Rafaello Busoni. Bobbs-Merrill, 1958. (2-4)

In the Great Walled Country of the frozen north, there
lived only children.   At Christmas time Grandfather Christmas visited the Great Walled Country first, since it was
quite close to his home.   He would leave gifts in the forest
for the children to find and give to others.   One year the
Country was visited by a stranger who appeared to be very
wise.   He scoffed at the traditional Christmas customs and
pointed out how much better it would be if each child chose
gifts for himself instead of for others as they went to the
forest.   The King therefore proclaimed that in the future no
one should gather gifts for anyone but himself.   Now, in the
same country lived a little boy named Inge, who cared for
his crippled sister.   Since she could not go into the forest,
he ignored the proclamation and gathered gifts only for her
instead of himself.   The other children, to their dismay,
found the forest empty of gifts, even though Inge found more
beautiful things than he had ever found before.   A visit to
Father Christmas by a town delegation soon revealed that the
advice of the "wise" man was poor advice indeed.

Activity

Sculptured objects and characters from "glue bread."
Tree ornaments of the characters from The Christmas Tree
Forest or of the gifts the children might have found there
can be made from "glue bread," which is a very permanent
modeling material.   Using one slice of fresh bread per pupil,
tear the bread into small pieces on a sheet of waxed paper.
Add about a tablespoon of glue to the bread and turn and
knead the mixture with the fingers.   It will be sticky at first,
so keep kneading until it is smooth (about fifteen minutes).
When it is smooth and pliable it is ready to mold into small
figures from the story, miniature models of gifts to be hung
on the tree or small trees for a miniature table model of
the "Christmas Tree Forest."   Food coloring or water color
can be added to the compound while mixing it, or figures can
be painted when completely dry.

Bailey, Carolyn Sherwin.   Miss Hickory (Chapter Nine:
    "Now Christmas Comes").   Illus. by Ruth Gannett.
    MacMillan, 1946.   (2-4)
        Miss Hickory is a doll fashioned from an apple wood
twig with a hickory nut head.   She is a "no-nonsense" kind
of doll and thinks that squirrel is making up fanciful tales
when he tells her of the wondrous things that happen in the
barn each Christmas Eve.   She ignores squirrel's tale and

goes to bed as usual, only to be awakened by the sound of
carols. Since this is, indeed, a strange sound to be hearing
in the woods which surround the deserted farmhouse, Miss
Hickory decided to investigate. She finds (and joins) a strange
animal procession which enters the barn where strange and
wonderful things do happen, but Miss Hickory's hard-headed-
ness keeps her from seeing the most wondrous thing of all.

Activity (1)

The legend that animals can speak on Christmas Eve
is an old one. Students will enjoy browsing through collections of Christmas stories to find other stories where animals talk. Good choices to have available are: Harald Wiberg's Christmas at the Tomten's Farm, Edith Hurd's Christmas Eve, and Astrid Lindgren's Christmas in the Stable.
Either individually or in groups, students should have the opportunity to retell the story they have found.
If it is possible to use one side of the classroom or a
long portion of the hall, students might construct a talking
animal procession. VERY LARGE animal figures can be
drawn on large poster roll paper, outlined with black, felt
tip markers, painted or decorated with a variety of scraps
of material, and mounted on the wall with loops of masking
tape. Such an animal procession could lead to the classroom door (if mounted in the hall) and from there to a manger scene. Using cut out, balloon-shaped captions, each
animal can be given something appropriate to say. Students
should develop their own captions and letter them in large
letters.

Activity (2)

What children do not enjoy creating dolls from natural
objects such as corncobs, twigs, nuts and apples? An autumn collecting trip can furnish a classroom with a variety of
doll-making activities. Acorns, seed-pods, nuts of all shapes
and sizes, sweet gum balls, dried fruits or whatever your
area affords can be collected. A Christmas manger scene
(with Miss Hickory present this time!) can be planned right
after Thanksgiving. Using the materials gathered, encourage
the children to create animals of any species. Some would-
be carpenters in your classroom can construct a miniature
barn using hay or dried grasses for the floor. As animals
are completed they can be placed about the barn looking at
a miniature creche. Plan a display area large enough to
hold every child's animal. It will grow as long as materials

are available (all inspired by this story which so effortlessly stimulates the creative use of natural building materials).

Bolognese, Don. A New Day. Illus. by the author. Dela-
    corte, 1973. (3-6)
        Mexican migrant workers, following the crops, arrive in the South searching for a place to stay. They find shelter in a gas station garage and are joined by a group of traveling musicians. The woman gives birth during the night and the poor people of the town bring gifts. Because of the crowds and the excitement, the sheriff orders the arrest of the couple. Through friends, however, they are warned in time to leave town so that trouble can be avoided.

Activity--Primary

        Students might be led to compare this story with the story of the Christ Child. Both similarities and differences can be noted. Perhaps a visit to the class from a person of a different culture or country might be arranged, so that children can see the different ways in which Christmas can be celebrated.

Activity--Intermediate

        Students can do their own illustrated version of this story to present to others as a holiday program. A slide show using color-lift slides selected from pictures in old magazines and narrated by several students can provide a thoughtful holiday program.

Briggs, Raymond. Father Christmas. Illus. by the author.
    Coward, McCann & Geoghegan, 1973. (4-6)
        Raymond Briggs introduces a Father Christmas who hates winter, ice, sleet, snow, cold, work, chimneys, soot, and even some of the snacks children leave for him on Christmas Eve! As he grumbles along his rounds he has trouble with television aerials, stairs, lighthouses and cats. By the time he returns to the North Pole, unhitches and feeds his reindeer and enjoys a shower and dry socks, he is ready for his ale and a big dinner. Of course, on his travels he has caught a cold, so a bit more wine with his dinner seems appropriate ... and then to bed and a well deserved rest.

Activity

This book might be introduced to creative writing
classes along with Mendoza's A Wart Snake in a Fig Tree
as examples of the parody as a literary style.   Certainly
there are those who may not appreciate the idea of doing a
parody based on Christmas music or the traditional image of
Santa Claus.   However, both of these are good examples of
the way an author can poke fun at time-worn customs.   Imagine, for example, Santa tangling with a television antenna
(which is, in fact, quite logical in this age).   Students may
enjoy examining some of the non-religious aspects of the holiday season in light of the modern society in which we live,
and themselves developing a simple parody: for example,
what might happen if the Food & Drug Administration recalled all candy canes (or turkeys, or cranberries) from the
stores just before Christmas?

Brown, Margaret Wise.   The Little Fir Tree.   Illus. by
    Barbara Cooney.   Crowell, 1954.   (K-2)
    The little fir tree was only one tiny part of the huge
forest, but had a special role to play in bringing happiness
to a lame boy.   During its seventh winter, a man carefully
dug all around the tree until it would be lifted out of the
ground, roots and all.   The tree was planted in a large
wooden tub, decorated, and placed in the lame child's bedroom.   Each spring it was returned to the forest and planted
once again.   Then, one winter, the tree was not moved, for
the little boy, who was now able to walk, led his friends to
the forest to decorate the tree as brightly as ever.

Activity

Talk with the children about the possibility of having
a live (rather than a cut) Christmas tree.   Are there advantages to having a live tree?   If you lived in a big city
apartment house would there be a place to plant the tree
after Christmas?   What would happen to the tree if it re-
mained in a wooden tub?   Students may want to visit the library to find out more about Christmas trees and where they
grow.   If possible, invite someone to the classroom who is
knowledgeable about plants and trees, to talk with the children about "Christmas tree farms" and how new trees are
planted each year to replace those which are cut.   Advice
can be given, too, on caring for a Christmas tree to keep it
fresh and to avoid the danger of fire.

Brown, Michael.   Santa Mouse.   Illus. by Elfreida DeWitt.
    Grosset & Dunlap, 1966.   (K-2)
        Little mouse was the only mouse in the big house
where he lived.   He spent his time daydreaming of the play-
mates he would like to have.   He treasured only one thing
which he had saved throughout the year--a piece of cheese.
On Christmas Eve he carefully wrapped up the cheese as a
gift for Santa, but the best gift of all was the one little
mouse received, a new job as Santa's helper, and a new
name ... Santa Mouse!

Activity

        By Christmas time, first grade students (who will es-
pecially enjoy this story) will be familiar enough with beginning and ending consonants to enjoy making new words from
SANTA MOUSE.   Print SANTA MOUSE in large letters on the
chalkboard.   Write the letters AN underneath.   Ask the children what letters in the name SANTA MOUSE could be used
to make new words using the letters AN.   Some responses
might be TAN, MAN, ANT, ANN.   Choose two more letters;
for example, OM.   Let the children make new words with
these letters using only letters found in SANTA.   Encourage
the children to find other letters which will make new words.

Alternate Activity

        Ask each child to choose an animal he or she might
like to be.   If Santa were to visit that animal, what kind of
gift might he bring?   What gift would the animal give to
Santa?   Children might want to keep their animal name a
secret and draw a picture of the gift their animal might give
to or receive from Santa.   Other children can guess from
seeing the picture of the gift what animal each child has decided to be.

Brown, Palmer.   Something for Christmas.   Illus. by the
    author.   Harper & Row, 1958.   (all ages)
        A small mouse has a hard time thinking of what he
can make or give for Christmas until his mother helps him
to see that love is the greatest gift of all.

Activity

        The simple dialogue in this tiny book lends itself to
dramatic reproduction.   Two children can easily learn the

dialogue, and with the addition of pointed paper cup noses
bedecked with pipe cleaner whiskers, a couple of cardboard
ears and a yarn tail, the scene is set for a pre-Christmas
sharing.   What a delight it would be for older students to
form a "touring company" of Something for Christmas and
travel to the other classrooms in the school to present this
delightful story.

Caudill, Rebecca. A Certain Small Shepherd. Illus. by
      William Pene DuBois.   Holt, Rinehart & Winston, 1965.
      (all ages)
           Jamie, mute from birth, is overjoyed when he is
chosen for the part of the shepherd in the school pageant.
Christmas Eve in Appalachia brings a severe snow storm
which causes cancellation of the pageant. Jamie is heart-
broken. A young couple comes to the cabin seeking shelter
from the storm and Jamie takes part in a miracle which
more than compensates for his disappointment.

Activity

           Children might interpret this story for others at
Christmastime through oral reading accompanied by appropriate color-lift slides.   Color-lift slides can be made from
pictures in clay-based magazines and clear contact paper.
2x2 slide mounts for mounting the slides can be purchased
at any photo supply store.   Photographic slides of the children's own illustrations can be made using a copy stand and
camera with slide film.   Appropriate background music can
be selected to accompany the reading and slides.

Chafetz, Henry. The Legend of Befana. Illus. by Ronni
      Solbert.   E. M. Hale & Co., 1963.   (2-4)
           An elderly widow, Befana, lived in Judea 2,000 years
ago. She had only her donkey for company. She heard of
the birth of the King of the Jews through the wise men who
passed her way. She put gifts on the back of her donkey
and tried to follow them. She was unable to find them, however. Her search took her as far away as Rome and she
decided to give her gifts to the poor children there. Thus,
Twelfth Night was begun and continues to this day.

Activity

           Ask for a volunteer from your classroom to do some

research on Twelfth Night and on Christmas customs in Italy.
Post a map of the Holy Land and the Mediterranean area so
that the class can see how far Befana and her donkey had to
travel to get to Rome.   Have one or more children figure
out how far it was in miles and the possible routes she might
have taken.   Have each of the children write or tell how they
think she got there.   (Fantasy accepted!)

Chaneles, Sol. Santa Makes a Change. Illus. by Jerome
    Snyder. Parents Magazine Press, 1970. (K-2)
        After wearing the same red outfit for hundreds of
years, Santa decides he needs a new suit. Jack Frost, the
elves and the reindeer agree and accompany Santa to the
store where he tries on outfits that make him become a band-
leader, a Scotsman with a kilt, a spaceman, a policeman,
Davy Crockett, a railroad engineer, a Swiss guard, a cow-
boy, a Chinese mandarin, an Indian chief, a ship's captain
and a cook. But, of course, no outfit looks quite right until
Santa once again dons his red suit.

Activity

        Tell the class that the famous clothing designers
throughout the world are both men and women. Perhaps
Santa does need a new outfit and a future famous clothing
designer could be right here in this classroom. If possible,
give the children dittoed outline pictures of Santa wearing
bathing trunks. Let each child design a new outfit for Santa
(it does not have to be red and white). Display Santa's new
wardrobe for all to see.

Duvoisin, Roger. Petunia's Christmas. Illus. by the author.
    Alfred A. Knopf, 1952. (K-2)
        Petunia, Mr. Pumpkin's pet goose, makes friends with
Charles, a goose on a neighboring farm who is being fattened
up for Christmas. Petunia's first plan to help Charles escape fails, but when she discovers that 20-pound Charles is
worth 75 cents a pound, she is determined to raise the money
to buy his freedom. She is so enterprising (and successful)
that Charles gains his freedom. Petunia and Charles are
married on Christmas Day.

Activity

        Read the story aloud to the point where Petunia de-

cides to earn the money to buy Charles' freedom.   Divide
the class into groups of three to five children.   Ask each
group to confer quietly and decide how Petunia might earn
the money.   If any student can determine the exact amount
of money to be raised (. 75 x 20), have the student tell the
class and show how the amount was figured (. 75 x 20 =
$15. 00).   If students are not able to figure the total, tell
them what it would be.

After groups have decided on how Petunia would raise
$15. 00, have a spokesman for each group tell what was de-
cided.   Let the class decide whether the scheme is practical
or not.   Finish reading the story.   Did any group guess how
Petunia earned the money?   Were any of the groups' ideas
better than the author's?   Help the children to see that an
author can choose from many possibilities when writing a
story.

Ets, Marie Hall and Aurora, Labastida.   Nine Days to Christ-
      mas.   Illus. by Marie Hall Ets.   Viking Press, 1959.
      (3-6)
      Ceci looks forward with eager anticipation to the "po-
sadas," the parties given on each night nine days before
Christmas.   The preparations of her family for the celebration and the choosing of her own piñata are events which are
delightfully told.   Bright, bold illustrations enhance the text.

Activity

This is an excellent book to use in a study of Christmas celebrations in other lands.   Many customs of Mexico
are explained in the text and pictures, with special emphasis
on the piñata, which can be almost any size or shape.   What
fun children can have making their own piñata (or one large
class piñata) filled with students' poems which convey holiday
wishes for others.   One very helpful book on the construction
of piñatas is Virginia Brock's Piñatas (Abingdon, 1966).   If
more than one classroom enters into the spirit of the posada,
class piñatas could be exchanged, with members of one class
receiving the Christmas wishes of another class.

Francoise.   Noel for Jeanne Marie.   Illus. by the author.
      Charles Scribner's Sons, 1953.   (K-2)
      In this story for the very youngest, Jeanne Marie
tells Patapon, the lamb, of the coming of Noel, the birthday
of Jesus.   She dreams aloud of the gifts Father Noel might

leave her in her wooden shoes, while Patapon bemoans the
fact that since he cannot remove his shoes there will be no
gift for him.   Jeanne Marie buys wooden shoes for Patapon
and both receive special gifts from Father Noel.

Activity

        Explain to the children that Christmas is celebrated
all over the world and that in the country of France (far
across the sea) the word for Christmas is Noel.   Write on
the chalkboard the word, Christmas, in the following languages: English--Christmas, French--Noel, Spanish--Navidad.
Pronounce the words for the children, having them repeat
after you.   A small group of eager researchers may want to
visit the school library and with the help of the librarian find
the word for Christmas in other languages.   If books based
on Christmas in other lands are available, borrow these for
display on the classroom reading table and allow plenty of
browsing time.

Hader, Berta and Elmer.   Reindeer Trail, a Long Journey
        From Lapland to Alaska.   Illus. by the authors.   Mac-
        millan, 1959.   (3-6)
        This is a simply told story of a true event in history.
By 1890, many Eskimos in Alaska were starving.   Indis-
criminate killing of the whales, caribou, and other Alaskan
wildlife by foreign hunters had depleted the herds to danger-
ously low levels.   An American, Sheldon Jackson, with the
approval of the United States government, went to Lapland to
buy and transport reindeer to Alaska.   The reindeer were accompanied by Lapp herders, who made the long and difficult
journey to teach the Eskimos how to care for the herds so
that hunger would never again threaten.   This is the story
of that journey.

Activity

        If the story is used with middle grade students, one
child might trace the journey on a map after the story is
read.   If a transparency of a world outline map is available
it can be projected and the student can mark the route with
grease pencil directly on the transparency.   This will wipe
clean after use.   As students hear the story ask them to list
the kinds of wildlife found in Alaska (bear, moose, walrus,
seal, whale, fish, caribou).   The class can be divided into
small groups and each group assigned one animal as a re-

search project. Students should be able to find a description
of the animal and other information about it such as: its
habits, any unusual information, whether or not it is in danger of extinction today and what might be done to conserve
wildlife. Reports can be presented to other members of the
class in a variety of ways--oral, written, dramatized, taped
or through simple illustrations on write-on filmstrip film.

Haywood, Carolyn. A Christmas Fantasy. Illus. by Glenys
    and Victor Ambrus. Morrow, 1972. (all ages)
        Was Santa Claus ever a child? Carolyn Haywood uses
this idea to create a fantasy about the childhood of Santa
Claus. He first appears as a baby on Christmas Day at the
home of a good woman who becomes his Godmother. As he
grows he discovers the joy of giving and receiving presents,
and decides that when he grows up he will be a "present
giver." Claus's strange habit of entering homes only through
chimneys comes in handy in his chosen career, as does his
wide girth and merry smile.

Activity

        This bright fantasy can open many doors to creative
thought. Children have probably never speculated on the possibility that Santa might once have been a child. Speculation
on other aspects of Christmas lore that are taken for granted
can lead to the writing of the students' own Christmas fan-
tasies. List on the chalkboard ideas that might be explored.
Students might wonder how Santa met Mrs. Claus or how he
found the elves to man his workshop, why are there no lady
elves, or what might happen if the reindeer went on strike on
Christmas Eve. The possibilities are endless.

Hoban, Russell. The Mole Family's Christmas. Illus. by
    Lillian Hoban. Parents Magazine Press, 1969. (1-3)
        "Harley Mole and his son Delver did straight mole
work. They tunneled and they dug and they brought home
the groceries." So begins the delightful story of the indus-
trious mole family whose days and nights are filled with work
and whose major excitement in life is to avoid being eaten
by Ephraim the Owl. One evening when Delver had finished
his chores he walked up to the "people house" to ask the
house mouse about Christmas. He learned that Christmas
is different things to different people (or animals) and that
one might receive gifts from a man in a red suit if one wrote

a letter and owned a chimney.   With this astonishing news
the mole family decides to build a chimney and write a letter asking for a telescope so that they might be able some
night to see the stars.   A happy tale sure to delight both
readers and listeners.

Activity

Be sure the children understand that one characteristic
of the mole is its poor eyesight.   Because of this characteristic, the telescope seems quite a logical gift.   Ask students
to volunteer information concerning characteristics of other
animals.   Some students may know that snakes shed their
skins every spring, or that beavers build their homes under
water, etc.   It may be necessary to have a number of simple
animal books sent to the classroom from the school library
and to allow time for the children to browse through these until more animal characteristics are found.   Both the animal
names and their unusual characteristics can be listed on the
chalkboard.   Let each child choose one animal and think of a
gift that would be appropriate for that animal.   The children
may either draw a picture of the gift or find and cut out a
picture of the gift from newspapers or old magazines and
place it next to the name and/or picture of the animal he or
she has chosen.   All pictures can be put together into a
class book entitled BEASTLY GIFTS and placed in the school
library for others to enjoy during the Christmas season.
Suggestions to start children thinking:
1. Since a snake sheds its skin each spring, it might
     welcome a raincoat or umbrella.
2. Since bears sleep (or hibernate) all winter, they might
     welcome extra warm pajamas.
3. Since the female cardinal is not as bright and colorful
     as the male, she might welcome a make-up kit, or a
     new hat, or feather brighteners.

Hopkins, Lee Bennett.   Sing Hey for Christmas Day!   Illus.
    by Laura Jean Allen.   Harcourt, Brace, Jovanovich,
    1975.   (all ages)
    Here are Christmas poems packaged for the most
choosy reader and tied together with sprightly green and
white illustrations.   Lee Hopkins has chosen from the works
of many well-known poets to gather a collection which ranges
from solemn scenes at the crèche to the joy of giving and
receiving gifts.

Activity

When a poem is committed to memory it becomes a lifetime companion.   Encourage each student to learn at least one poem from this or other Christmas collections.   A poetry sharing time can be just the thing to bring calm and reflectiveness to children bursting with pre-holiday excitement. Ask students to be ready to share their favorite poem the week before the holidays begin.   Devoting the last few minutes of each day to a sharing of poems by students will bring a happy note to the day's end.

Hurd, Edith Thacher.   Christmas Eve.   Illus. by Clement
    Hurd.   Harper & Row, 1962.   (all ages)
    This simple but effective telling of the journey and arrival of the animals at the stable on Christmas Eve has the flavor of a tone poem.   The mood is gentle and reflective and the story borrows from the ancient beliefs of country people concerning the ability of animals to speak on Christmas Eve, as well as the blooming of the white rose outside the stable door on that cold winter's night when Christ was born.

Activity--Primary

If students construct a manger scene in the classroom this would be a perfect book to read just before the scene is completed.   Children will want to add to the scene those creatures which are a part of the legend but which are not usually found there: the wren, the cock, the duck, the raven, the honeybee and the reindeer.

Activity--Intermediate

This story lends itself well to puppetry.   Stick puppets can be made of each wild creature and used to act out the story against a stable door backdrop as the story is read aloud.

Hutchins, Pat.   The Silver Christmas Tree.   Illus. by the
    author.   Macmillan, 1974.   (K-3)
    Squirrel used all of the beautiful things he could find in the forest to decorate his Christmas tree, holly and ivy, berries and pine cones, and even mistletoe.   He worked all day but his great surprise came that night when he discovered

that his beautiful tree was topped by a gleaming silver star
that HE had not put there.   But alas, the next morning the
star was gone and squirrel suspected that his friends were
hiding it from him.   As the friends exchange their gifts
throughout the day squirrel does not find his star, but when
night comes, he discovers that he has a gift to give, too.
The silver star appears once more!

Activity

        Make a simple outline pattern of a Christmas tree
which can be dittoed and given to each student.   Tree patterns should be cut out and glued to poster board.   Ask students to bring from home discarded items such as yarn,
scraps of material, buttons, sequins, etc.   Using these items
as well as scraps of colored construction paper, let each
child decorate his tree.   As each tree is finished, the child
can receive a silver star (cut from aluminum foil) to staple
to the top of his tree.   Imagination should be encouraged and
all trees displayed on the classroom bulletin board.

Kahl, Virginia.   Plum Pudding for Christmas.   Illus. by the
        author.   Scribner's, 1956.   (K-2)
        This long-time favorite story in rhyme tells of a Duke
who left his castle to do battle just before Christmas.   The
Duchess and their 13 daughters were lonely without him, so
they invited the King to have Christmas dinner with them.
He accepted, with one stipulation: they must have plum pud-
ding--"If you serve a pudding ... and that pudding is plum.
Plums that are purple, plums in a clump, so that each bumpy
lump is a plum that is plump."   But little Brunhilde spoiled
the preparations by eating the only plums available.   Great
dismay followed, for the King was expecting his plum pudding!
The day is saved when the Duke appears, home from battle,
with a sack of big purple plums.   Everyone enjoys the pudding feast.

Activity

        A delightful plum pudding can be concocted very simp-
ly in your classroom (if you have a portable oven that can
be brought to school or a cafeteria oven is made available
for baking).   Mix one large can of plums with one box of
yellow or white cake mix (do not add water or eggs).   Bake
for 25 minutes at 350 degrees.   Each child can sample a little of the plum pudding for his treat at lunchtime.   (For more
pudding, make more cakes!)

Keats, Ezra Jack. <u>The Little Drummer Boy</u>. Macmillan,
    1968. (all ages)
    Bright yellows, oranges, reds and blues dance across
each page of Ezra Jack Keats' beautiful illustrations of this
well-loved Christmas song. The young drummer boy has an
almost impish look as he cavorts with the ox and the lamb
and other creatures as he approaches the manger to give to
the Christ Child the only gift he has ... his ability to play
the drum.

Activity

This beautiful book is available as a sound filmstrip
from Weston Woods in Weston, Conn. It would be a very
desirable permanent addition to the school's audiovisual collection for it can be enjoyed again and again by children of
all ages. Children will enjoy learning the song in music
class and singing along with the filmstrip. If the filmstrip
is not available, try showing the pictures on the opaque pro-
jector as the children sing. It will be a shared experience
not soon forgotten.

Kent, Jack. <u>Jack Kent's Twelve Days of Christmas</u>. Illus.
    by the author. Parents Magazine Press, 1973. (all
    ages)
    In this amusing version of the old song, Jack Kent
interprets the verses literally. For example, on the second
day of Christmas the "true love" receives TWO partridges,
two pear trees and two turtle doves. By the fourth day of
Christmas the "true love" has accumulated four partridges,
four pear trees, six turtle doves, six French hens and four
collie birds. By the twelfth day of Christmas the number of
gifts is so vast that they cannot all be shown on one page
and the "true love" goes into hiding to avoid receiving any
more gifts.

Activity

After laughing together over the accumulated treasures
ask the children to compute how many items the "true love"
actually received. A chart on the chalkboard similar to the
one here will help in the computation.

Item	Quantity	Number of Days Received	Total
partridge	1	12	12

turtle doves	2	11	22
French hens	3	10	30
collie birds	4	9	36
golden rings	5	8	40
geese	6	7	42
swans	7	6	42
maids	8	5	40
pipers	9	4	36
drummers	10	3	30
lords	11	2	22
ladies	12	1	12

Total Number of gifts ——

Kingman, Lee.   The Magic Christmas Tree.   Illus. by Bet-
    tina.   Farrar, Straus & Cudahy, 1956.   (2-4)
        Joanna lived in a cottage near the woods.   Julie lived
in a mansion in the town.   Both little girls discover the same
pine tree in the forest and each, without knowing about the
other, pretended that the tree belonged to her.   As the girls
find objects which each has left under the tree, they begin to
think of the tree as magic.   When finally they meet, the
mystery of the objects is solved but each girl denies the other's claim to the tree.   The magic of the tree, however, is
revealed when the girls do discover the true meaning of
Christmas.

Activity

        Let each child bring a shoe box to school which can
be decorated using a Christmas motif.   Divide the class into
pairs, but do not tell each child who his partner is.   Give
each child the name of another child in this class.   This is
to be his "secret pal."   (Secret pals will have each other's
names but the children are not to know this.)   Several days
before the holidays each secret pal should find an opportunity to secretly put some gift he has made in the other's box.
This could be a poem, drawing, etc.   The day before vacation, secret pals should try to guess who they are.   Children should be surprised to find that the person for whom
they made a gift was the same person who made a gift for
them.

Lindgren, Astrid.   The Tomten.   (adapted from a poem by
    Victor Rydberg.)   Illus. by Harald Wiberg.   Coward,
    1961.   (all ages)

The lyrical quality of the text, combined with the soft, almost veiled illustrations, tells the story of a soft-footed visitor, the Tomten, who every night visits an old farm, talking to the animals in a Tomten language. His words are words of hope and comfort, for he is the spirit of well-being which covers the farm and all who live there.

Activity--Primary

Small children often equate the Tomten with Santa Claus because of his red cap and beard. Before sharing the book, the teacher or librarian might talk briefly about the "little people" of different countries, equating the Tomten with an elf. After sharing the story, ask the children for suggestions as to the kind of "silent little language" the Tomten used. Children will enjoy making up their own Tomten language and trying it out on each other. This might be a pantomime language where the message is acted out, or a code language where a gesture stands for a letter or word.

Activity--Intermediate

Older students may want to discover more about the "little people," their names, country of origin, a description and the particular magic powers given to them in the folklore. Information gathered could be the basis for an attractive and informative bulletin board.

McGinley, Phyllis. How Mrs. Santa Claus Saved Christmas. Illus. by Kurt Wurth. Lippincott, 1963. (K-3)
The story of how Santa Claus couldn't get along without Mrs. Santa is told in rollicking verse accompanied by bright, happy illustrations. It is Mrs. Santa, of course, who tells Santa what to bring to the children each year, and she is never wrong when she makes her suggestions. However, one year the things that she suggests seem so ridiculous to Santa that he refuses to do as she asks. So Mrs. Santa, being quite resourceful in her own right, lets Santa oversleep on Christmas Eve and takes the sleigh out herself. Imagine Santa's horror when he finds, on her return, that she has deliberately mixed up all the gifts and that each child received something totally different from what he expected ("skis for Bookworms, books for the Baseball Breed"). Santa is sure he is in disgrace until the laughter of children around the world turns to cheers because they have received the wishes "of their hearts they had never told."

Activity

Introduce a "What Would Happen If" game to the children. Stimulate creative thought and imagination by starting the game with "What would happen if you received a computer for Christmas?" Let those children who can think of an answer raise their hands, and call on one of them. After that child has given his answer, ask him or her to think of another "What would happen if" for another child to answer. Try to avoid having the same children called on more than once so that all children have a chance to respond.

Mendoza, George. A Wart Snake in a Fig Tree. Illus. by
  Etienne Delessert. Dial Press, 1968. (4-6)
This parody of "The Twelve Days of Christmas" is filled with absurd lines and illustrations. "On the first day of Christmas my true love gave to me a wart snake in a fig tree" is the opening line of this familiar Christmas song. As the text and illustrations progress, the "true love" receives such gems as "two bags of soot, three cobwebs, four raven wings, five useless things," etc. Each "gift" is appropriately illustrated in bold, full-page illustrations.

Activity

This book can serve as an excellent introduction to the literary form known as the parody, in which an author's or composer's original work has been changed, usually to achieve a comic effect. The changes made, however, are not so complete as to preclude recognition of the original work. Students might enjoy taking other non-religious Christmas or holiday songs and developing their own parody. If the class has a guitarist or pianist the song might be sung for the class ... or it can be sung without accompaniment. A word of caution: if a holiday song is chosen for the parody, care should be taken that the basic values of the holiday are not distorted so as to cause listeners to take offense.

Miller, Edna. Mousekin's Christmas Eve. Illus. by the author. Prentice-Hall, 1965. (K-3)
Mousekin finds himself alone in a cold, empty house and knows he must undertake a dangerous journey to find a new home. His trip through the snow is filled with suspense, as the wind and the cold and the sounds and unexpected movements of other animals add to his fears. Suddenly Mousekin

finds himself surrounded by circles of color and discovers
that the color is coming from the window of a house.   His
joy and delight are unbounded, and squeezing through a crack
in the window, he discovers a magnificent tree with lights
and good things to eat.   His joy is complete as he finally
finds a safe haven in the peaceful manger scene.

Activity

      Ask the children if it might be possible to have a
beautiful Christmas tree without purchasing a single ornament.   (The good things Mousekin found to eat on the tree
should give children a clue.)   Let children suggest types of
decorations which might adorn such a tree.   If trees are allowed in the school, children might want to try out their
ideas in decorating a classroom tree.   Popcorn can be popped
and strung on thread along with whole, uncooked cranberries.
Ornaments can be made with "Creative Clay" to decorate the
class tree until Christmas vacation.   Then each child can
take his ornament home to decorate the family tree.
      The recipe for Creative Clay is as follows: In a
saucepan stir thoroughly one cup of corn starch and two cups
of (one-pound package) baking soda.   Mix in 1 1/4 cups of
cold water.   Heat, stirring constantly until mixture reaches
a slightly moist, mashed-potato consistency.   Turn out on a
plate and cover with a damp cloth.   When cool enough to
handle, knead like bread dough.   Shape as desired or store
tightly covered for later use.
      To shape creative clay, form with the hands or roll
out to a 1/4-inch thickness and cut with a knife or cookie
cutter.   If desired, trim with bits of clay, moistened and
pressed in place.   Pierce a hole near the edge for stringing
the ornament.   When dry, the clay can be painted with water
colors, poster paints, or felt tip pens.   Brush on clear nail
polish or shellac for a protective coating and shine if desired.

Moeri, Louise.   Star Mother's Youngest Child.   Illus. by
    Trina Schart Hyman.   Houghton-Mifflin, 1976.   (3-6)
      Star Mother's youngest child cannot be consoled.   His
dearest wish is to celebrate just one Christmas on Earth before he must join the constellations.   When his wish is
granted he finds himself at the door of a hut where a poor old
woman, who often dreams of having a real Christmas, lives
all alone, forgotten by family and the townsfolk.   The appearance of the ugly child who seems to have no understanding of

the simplest things of life (like chores and turnips) profound-
ly changes the old woman's life.   Told in beautifully flowing
language, the story of the old woman and the boy comes so
alive through the author's skill that characters almost seem
to jump from the pages.

Activity

Louise Moeri draws word pictures for her readers
through the use of unusual and delightful similes.   Explain
to the children that a simile compares two or more things
using the words like or as.   Write on the chalkboard this
simile from the book: "The stars were twinkling and shim-
mering together like some great family of acrobats in silver
sequins. " Discuss the use of the simile in making word pictures.   Make the book available to interested children to see
if they can find more similes used by the author.   Let the
children write their own holiday similes: The tree glittered
like _____.   The red and white striped candy cane tasted
like _____.   Santa's beard was as long as _____, etc.

Szekeres, Cyndy.   A Christmas Party.   From a poem by
      Carolyn Sherwin Bailey.   Pantheon, 1975.   (K-2)
This beautifully illustrated poem tells of a Christmas
Eve party given by the forest for all of its inhabitants.
Squirrels, woodchucks, a bear disturbed from its slumbers,
foxes, rabbits and a host of other animals dance on the
"snowy rug" amidst "trees hung with frosty chains and pom-
poms. " The appearance of Santa with his gifts delights all
of the animals, not a one of whom "could hang a Christmas
stocking. "

Activity

This is a perfect Christmas poem for a class choral
reading.   The lines are short, simple and easy to remember,
and the reading can be done with individual children learning
separate lines, with perhaps the entire class joining in on the
first and last lines.   Children might enjoy doing their own
illustrations of the forest and its animals to show during the
reading.   Illustrations can be done individually or as a large
wall mural.   If a camera and copy stand are available, slides
can be taken of the illustrations and can be projected during
the reading.

Thayer, Jane. Gus Was a Christmas Ghost. Illus. by Sey-
    mour Fleishman. Morrow, 1969. (K-2)
    Mr. Frizzle, the manager of the historical museum
where Gus the Ghost lived, was invited to spend Christmas
in Florida. Following Mr. Frizzle's departure, Gus and
Cora, the cat, decide to have an old-fashioned Christmas
complete with a tree, a turkey and mince pie. As the celebration got underway Gus and Cora thought they heard burg-
lars. The burglar, however, turned out to be Mr. Frizzle,
whose bus was cancelled by a snowstorm. After Gus, Cora
and Mr. Frizzle celebrate a Christmas Eve together, they
do one last thing before going to bed--they hang up their
stockings!

Activity

    What might a ghost expect to find in his stocking on
Christmas morning? Since the book does not tell what Gus
received, this could lead to much speculation on the part of
the children. Ask each child to draw Gus's stocking and
show what will be in it on Christmas morning. Or draw one
very large stocking for the classroom bulletin board and ask
each child to draw and cut out one thing that Gus might like
to receive. These gifts would be mounted in and around the
large stocking.

Wiberg, Harald. Christmas at the Tomten's Farm. Illus.
    by the author. Coward-McCann, 1968. (3-6)
    This is a beautifully illustrated, highly detailed, de-
lightful account of a traditional Christmas celebration on a
Swedish farm. Rich in folklore and superstition, the story
tells of the family's preparations for and celebration of the
holiday. The juniper beer, making of the candles, black
pudding and sausages, the Christmas torch, the gifts and the
games are all observed by the Tomten, a silent, small creature who watches over the farm each night. Each Christmas
he receives payment for this task in the form of a bowl of
porridge. The book presents a marvelous opportunity for
sharing with students the Christmas customs and folklore of
another country.

Activity

    This story can be interpreted by students in many
ways. A large mural, a table display or a series of shoe-
box dioramas can retell the story visually. If shoe-box

dioramas are made, each student can select one scene from
the story to illustrate. If outside scenes are chosen, the
ground can be made with sand and rocks glued on modeling
clay which has been molded to the desired shape. Buildings
can be made from popsicle sticks which have been glued together and figures can be shaped from wire and covered with
cloth or fur material. An appropriate background can be
painted on the sides of the box and dioramas can be displayed
in the order in which scenes appeared in the story.

Christmas Through the Eyes of Laura Ingalls Wilder

        An entire Christmas pageant can be created based on
and inspired by the Laura Ingalls Wilder "Little House" books.
In this beautiful series, the author has written vividly and
accurately of the pioneer life of her family. Each book in
the series has a chapter or two about Christmas and how it
was celebrated on the frontiers of America in the 19th century. A totally different era comes to life for today's children through reading these first-hand accounts of the sacrifice, integrity and warm human values which shaped the back-
bone of our country. A view into Christmas long ago gives
children a deeper appreciation of the courage and resource-
fulness of their forefathers and a new view of the celebration
of Christmas today. The characters in Laura Ingalls Wilder's books are so real, so true to life, so authentic to the
times that the modern child can identify with them readily
while having an exciting glimpse into our country's history.
        If an entire school can be involved in a Christmas
Long Ago project, each classroom could focus on one book
in the Little House series. Examples of titles which could
be used by each grade level are as follows:

First Grade: Little House in the Big Woods (Harper 1953)
        The Ingalls family lived in a little log house in Wis-
consin in 1872, miles from any neighbors or settlements.
Christmas meant a peppermint stick and a rag doll with special goodies coming from the kitchen and relatives traveling
for many miles to join them.

Second Grade: Little House on the Prairie
        This book follows the Ingalls on their move by covered
wagon into Indian territory, to what is now Kansas. A new

log cabin was built and the family was settled in by winter.
But remoteness and bad weather promised little Christmas
for the children.   A neighbor risked his life so that stockings were not empty.   Each girl had a shiny tin cup of her
own, a stick of candy, a tiny cake, and a bright new penny.
There never had been such a Christmas!

Third Grade: On the Banks of Plum Creek
        Third graders will be amazed to learn that children
were willing to sacrifice having any Christmas at all so that
their Pa could have the horses he needed for plowing.   Christmas meant being unselfish.   When Pa was lost in a blizzard
the following year, he ate the crackers and candy which he
had been bringing home and the only Christmas celebration
was a can of oysters.   But having Pa survive was enough to
make the family happy and grateful.

Fourth Grade: By the Shores of Silver Lake
        In this book fourth graders will be interested in how

to file a homestead claim as the Ingalls family does. Life
has not been easy since the last book, for scarlet fever has
left Mary blind. The family experience their first ride on
a railroad and live in a rough railroad camp. But company
makes their lean Christmas a happy one, with small presents
on the breakfast table for the first time.

Fifth Grade: The Long Winter
        The Long Winter will make fifth graders shiver as
they try to picture what it would be like to be cut off from
all sources of supply for months during a series of blizzards.
Running out of food and fuel, the courageous family made a
Christmas out of ingenuity and love for one another. Reading
a magazine story was a celebration in itself. Finally in
May, when the trains were able to get through, a Christmas
barrel arrived with clothing and a turkey for a belated celebration.

Sixth Grade: Little Town on the Prairie
        Sixth graders will appreciate the coming of civiliza-
tion to the frontiers and the growing up of society, although
Christmas doesn't seem the same with the family beginning
to split up. Mary has gone away to school and Laura was
able to get her first job in town. At last Christmas meant
gifts for everyone and the final book, These Happy Golden
Years, tells of the candy, popcorn balls, oranges and gifts
which were a part of the celebration. Yet, the warmth of
love and loyalty, the music of Pa's fiddle and the unity of
the family all made Christmas a time of joy. The songs
Pa played are recorded in The Laura Ingalls Wilder Songbook
and all grades could learn some of the songs which cheered
the Ingalls family through both the difficult and bountiful
times.

Program Suggestions

        To make this a meaningful Christmas sharing project,
the books should be read aloud in every classroom. In each
class the children can share ideas of how best to interpret
the Christmas chapters of their book. Music, choral reading,
a narrator and pantomime, as well as actual dramatizations,
are all possibilities. The children will think of other ways
to present their scene. But no child will feel the same about
Christmas in America today after such an exposure to a true
account of Christmas yesterday.
        If this project is one for your classroom alone, use
whichever books are most appropriate for your grade level,

or read aloud the Christmas chapters in several books.   If
your students have been immersed in these books all fall,
for the Christmas season they may want to create three-dimensional scenes of Christmas long ago around the classroom.   Scenes can depict the Ingalls family each year or
small groups of children could take one of the books and
make a movie of the Christmas chapter.

By creating drawings in sequence on roll paper the
story can unfold as it is unrolled on one side of a box "stage"
and rolled up on the other side.   A narrator will be useful
to tie the "film" together.   If all books are used, Act I
could begin with Little House in the Big Woods and Act VII
end with These Happy Golden Years.   Every student could
become involved as an artist, projectionist, narrator, etc.

An intermediate class eager to do a Christmas dramatization will find that Farmer Boy is a natural.   For after
reading this story of Almanzo Wilder's growing up on a New
York State farm in the 1860s, the children will be anxious to
recreate how Christmas was celebrated at that time.   The
details of the preparations and execution of the holiday are
so vividly described that children could write dialogue and
action based on the setting, gaining a valuable view into the
past of a very different Christmas celebration than children
are exposed to today.

Bulletin Board Quiz

On the library or classroom bulletin board place a
paper Christmas tree (about 2 1/2 feet tall).   Beginning
twelve days before Christmas vacation put beside the tree a
Christmas question that can be answered if any child
has read the Christmas story from which the question is
taken.   The first child to answer the question each day can
make a paper ornament with his name on it to pin on the
tree.   If desired, you may want to limit the number of questions any one child can answer so that a single child does
not give all the answers.   After the question is answered
correctly, put the answer up beside the question for the re-
mainder of the day.   Don't make the questions too easy.
Encourage the children to browse in the library to find those
Christmas books they have not read.   (Titles should be suitable for the grade intended.)   The following questions are for
a library bulletin board and the contest is open to all children

in the school. A box is placed near the paper tree and students write their answers and the time of day and drop them in the box. The winner is announced at the end of each day.

1. Who stole Christmas? (Grinch)

2. What Christmas character needed a crutch? (Tiny Tim)

3. What gift did Santa Mouse give Santa Claus? (cheese)

4. The little fir tree was decorated with... (berries, apples, cookies)

5. What did the mole family get for Christmas? (telescope)

6. What happened to Petunia on Christmas day? (got married)

7. How did the Christmas whale help Santa? (carried his packages)

8. What happened to Jamie on Christmas day? (he spoke)

9. What did Jeanne Marie buy for Patapon? (shoes)

10. Where did Mousekin sleep on Christmas Eve? (in the manger)

11. What made squirrel's Christmas tree silver? (starlight)

12. What two girls each claimed the same pine tree? (Julie & Joanna)

CHRISTMAS TREE QUIZ

Christmas trees come in all shapes, sizes and places. Use the card catalog in your school and/or public library to complete these Christmas Tree titles.

1. Budbill, David. CHRISTMAS TREE ___Farm___. Macmillan, 1974.

2. Caton, Marion. FIRST CHRISTMAS TREE ON THE ___Moon___. Exposition, 1972.

3. Mendoza, George. CHRISTMAS TREE ___Alphabet___ BOOK. Watts, 1971.

4. Alden, Raymond. CHRISTMAS TREE ___Forest___ .
    Bobbs, 1958.

5. Estes, Eleanor. THE ___Coat Hanger___ CHRISTMAS
    TREE. Atheneum, 1973.

6. Green, Robert. THE ___Ebony___ TREE AND THE SPIR-
    IT OF CHRISTMAS. Exposition, 1975.

7. Knight, Hilary. ___Firefly___ IN A FIR TREE. Hough-
    ton-Mifflin, n. d.

8. Kraus, Robert. THE TREE THAT STAYED UP UNTIL
    ___Next Christmas___ . Dutton, n. d.

9. Laugeson, Mary. THE ___Chrisamat___ TREE. Bobbs,
    1970.

10. Mehler, Ed. THE ___Scrawny___ LITTLE TREE. Platt-
    Monk, 1973.

11. Rock, Gail. THE ___House___ WITHOUT A CHRISTMAS
    TREE. Knopf, 1974.

12. Uchida, Yoshiko. THE ___Forever___ CHRISTMAS TREE.
    Scribner's, 1963.

CHRISTMAS IN OTHER LANDS (gr. 4-6)

Many delightful stories have been written about Christmas as it is celebrated in other lands. Below are titles of
Christmas books you won't want to miss. Ask your teacher
to post a world map on the bulletin board in your classroom.
As you and your friends read some of these titles and discover the country in which a particular story takes place,
write the title of the book neatly on a strip of white paper.
Pin the title to the bulletin board near the map. Attach a
string from the title you have posted to another pin placed on
the country where the story takes place. See how many
countries you and your friends can reach before Christmas!

1. Ets, Marie Hall. Nine Days to Christmas. Viking,
    1959. (Mexico)

2. Francoise. Noel for Jeanne Marie. Scribner's, 1953.
    (France)

3. Lindgren, Astrid. Christmas in Noisy Village. Viking,
    1964. (Sweden)

4. Potter, Beatrix. <u>The Tailor of Gloucester</u>. Warne,
    1968. (England)

5. Robbins, Ruth. <u>Baboushka and the 3 Kings</u>. Parnas-
    sus, 1960. (Russia)

6. Bemelmans, Ludwig. <u>Hansi</u>. Viking, 1934. (Austria)

7. Butler, Suzanne. <u>Starlight in Tourrone</u>. Little, 1965.
    (France)

8. Sawyer, Ruth. <u>The Christmas Anna Angel</u>. Viking,
    1944. (Hungary)

9. Uchida, Yoshiko. <u>The Forever Christmas Tree</u>. Scrib-
    ner, 1963. (Japan)

10. Peterson, Hans. <u>Erik and the Christmas Horse</u>.
    Lothrop, 1970. (Sweden)

11. Dickens, Charles. <u>A Christmas Carol</u>. Lippincott,
    1952. (England)

12. Carlson, Natalie. <u>The Family Under the Bridge</u>.
    Harper, 1958. (France)

13. Balet, Jan. <u>A   Christmas Tale</u>.
    Delacorte, 1967. (Portugal)

14. DeBosschere, Jean and Morris. <u>Christmas Tales of
    _____</u>. Dover, 1972. (Flanders)

15. Kent, Jack. <u>Christmas Piñata</u>. Parents, 1975. (Mex-
    ico)

A CHRISTMAS FEAST

        Complete the book titles and find the missing foods in
the Christmas feast puzzle below.

Across

1. <u>Arthur's Christmas   </u>, by Lillian Hoban.
        Harper & Row, 1972.

3. <u>   for Christmas</u>, by Marguerite de Angeli.
        E. M. Hale, 1965.

4. <u>The Christmas   </u>, by Ruth Sawyer. Viking,
        1944.

Down

1. The Christmas _____ Sprinkle Snatcher, by Vip.
    Simon & Schuster, 1969.

2. _____ Journey, by Julia Cunningham.   Pantheon,
    1967.

5. Conscience _____ by E. Nesbit.   Coward-Mc-
    Cann, 1970.

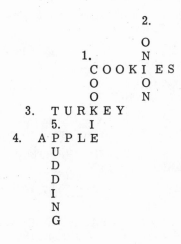

```
                                  2.
                                  O
                      1.          N
                       C O O K I  E S
                       O          O
                       O          N
              3.    T U R K E Y
              5.       I
          4.  A P P L E
                       U
                       D
                       D
                       I
                       N
                       G
```

MISSING CHRISTMAS ANIMALS

        Use the card catalog in your school or public library
to complete the following book titles.   Find the missing animals.   Unscramble the animal names and fill in the blanks.

OCW	OESMU	OEDNYK	TTRESO
RTEOOSR	SEARB	OESMU	LEMO
CITKEC	SACTSSUPY	OERSH	DIPRES
TCA	PPPYU	TTKNEI	NNUYB
LEAHW	PEELATNH	GIPTEL	BBARTI

1. AZOR AND THE BLUE EYED __Cow__ , by Maude Crowley. Walck, 1951.

2. THE __Cricket__ ON THE HEARTH, by Charles Dickens. Dutton, 1963.

3. THE CHRISTMAS __Whale__ , by Roger Duvoisin. Knopf, 1945.

4. LITTLE __Bear's__ CHRISTMAS, by Janice. Lothrop, 1964.

5. BABY __Elephant__ AND THE SECRET WISHES, by Sesyle Joslin. Harcourt, 1962.

6. THE __Puppy__ WHO WANTED A BOY, by Jane Thayer. Morrow, 1958.

7. THE CHRISTMAS __Mouse__ , by Elizabeth Wenning. Holt, Rinehart & Winston, 1959.

8. THE CHRISTMAS __Kitten__ , by Janet Konkle. Children's Press, 1953.

9. THE __Mole__ FAMILY'S CHRISTMAS, by Russell Hoban. Parents Magazine Press, 1969.

10. HOW __Spider__ SAVED CHRISTMAS, by Robert Kraus. Simon & Shuster, 1970.

11. THE CHRISTMAS __Bunny__ , by Will & Nicholas. Harcourt, 1953.

12. HOW A __Piglet__ CRASHED A CHRISTMAS PARTY, by Boris Zakhoder. Lothrop, 1971.

13. EMMET __Otter's__ JUGBAND CHRISTMAS, by Russell Hoban. Parents Magazine Press, 1971.

14. THE CHRISTMAS __Otters__ , by Glenn Balch. Crowell, 1970.

15. __Donkey__ FOR THE KING, by John and Patricia Beatty. Macmillan, 1966.

16. THE __Pussycat's__ CHRISTMAS, by Margaret Wise Brown. Crowell, 1949.

17. SANTA __Mouse__ , by Michael Brown. Grosset & Dunlap, 1966.

18. THE __Cat__ WHO KNEW THE MEANING OF CHRISTMAS, by Marion Gremmels. Augsburg, 1972.

19. HOW __Rabbit__ FOUND CHRISTMAS, by Laura Lee Hope. Wonder, n. d.

20. WISE __Rooster__ : EL GALLO SABIO, by Mariana Prieto. Day, 1962.

HANUKKAH

Background Information

The Feast of Lights, or Hanukkah, is an eight-day celebration of Jewish families to commemorate the victory of Judah Maccabee over Antiochus who had captured and defiled the Jewish Temple in Jerusalem. Judah Maccabee led his band of men against Antiochus and recaptured the Temple, discovering that the sacred lamp had only enough oil to burn for one day. Through a miracle of the light, however, it burned for eight days until the needed oil was found. Judah Maccabee and his followers declared this eight-day period a time of thanksgiving and praise, and thus Hanukkah is celebrated today, usually falling around the middle of December.

It is important for children to learn about customs different from their own in a way which generates respect. As they learn to understand the background and practices of many ethnic groups, tolerance and appreciation will grow. Teachers can help to eradicate the ignorance which breeds intolerance. Understanding and familiarity can come through exposure to good books and the activities they stimulate. All of the following books can trigger activities which help make memorable the customs of Hanukkah, a loved and cherished tradition of Jewish people all over the world.

Suggested Titles for Use	Suggested Grade Level
Chanover. Happy Hanukkah Everybody	K-2
Coopersmith. A Chanukah Fable for Christmas	K-2
Morrow. A Great Miracle--The Story of Hanukkah	2-5
Purdy. Jewish Holidays	all ages

Suggested Titles for Use	Suggested Grade Level
Simon. Hanukkah	2-4
Taylor. More All of a Kind Family	4-6

Chanover, Hyman and Alice. Happy Hanukkah Everybody.
    Illus. by Maurice Sendak. United Synagogue Commission
    on Jewish Education, 1954. (K-2)
        This bright picture book tells of the first-night cele-
bration of Hanukkah in a home with three children. Maurice
Sendak's lively illustrations enhance the simple but delightful
story of a happy family custom. The words and music of
several Hanukkah songs and blessings are included. The one
in English could readily be learned in younger grades. The
Hebrew ones might be a fun challenge for older classes.

Coopersmith, Jerome. A Chanukah Fable for Christmas.
    Illus. by Syd Hoff. G. P. Putnam's Sons, 1969. (K-2)
        This is a whimsical rhyming story of a little boy's
dream which weaves Christmas and Chanukah together. To
appreciate the little boy's longing for a Santa Claus and the
fulfillment of his wishes, the class should have some background of what Chanukah is and how it is celebrated by Jewish families. An explanation of the six-pointed star, a dreydl, and a soldier hat above a patched eye would be helpful.
The humorous tale has a happy ending and stirs an appreciation that all peoples of the world celebrate holidays differently and "That's what makes the world good" ... for "Who
would ask for a garden where flowers all match?"

Morrow, Betty. A Great Miracle--The Story of Hanukkah.
    Illus. by Howard Simon. Harvey House, 1968. (2-5)
        The heroic tale of the Jews' victory over the Syrians
is written here with style and rhythm. Taken from the
Apocrypha of the Bible, this story, which is behind the festival of Hanukkah, is retold with Biblical strength and vigor.
The beautiful pen drawings which accompany the text depict
clearly the scenes and actions of the times. The historical
background and current customs of the holiday are also explained. All children will benefit from exposure to this great
epic of the Western world.

Purdy, Susan Gold. Jewish Holidays--Facts, Activities and

Crafts.   J. B. Lippincott, 1969.   (for teachers at all
levels)
     This useful book contains a clear explanation of the
background, history and modern traditions of the festival of
Hanukkah, including a description of Tel Aviv and why it is
called the "City of Lights" during Hanukkah.   The little money
gifts for children (Hanukkah gelt), the ceremony of lighting
the candles on the menorah, the games to be played with a
dreydl are all described with clarity.   Detailed drawings and
explanations are given for the making of a clay menorah.
This would take a bit of time if it is to be used in a Hanukkah celebration, for the clay must harden.   An easier project for children in a classroom would be the making of a
dreydl box.   A list of materials which are readily available
in most classrooms and carefully executed diagrams and descriptions, including a full-sized pattern, make this an appealing individual activity for many ages.

Simon, Norma.   Hanukkah.   Illus. by Symeon Shimin.
     Crowell, 1966.   (2-4)
     This is a simply written account of the historical
background and modern customs of this Jewish holiday.   The
text also includes the ancient legend of Hanukkah, retold with
power and simplicity.   Reverence and respect shine through
both words and pictures.   The book concludes with a com-
ment on the rights of Americans to freedom of religion, re-
ferring to the letter George Washington wrote to the first
Jewish immigrants assuring them that they could worship as
they pleased in the United States.

Taylor, Sydney.   More All of a Kind Family.   Illus. by
     Mary Stevens.   Follett, 1954.   (4-6)
     This is the continuing story of a New York immigrant
Jewish family in the early days of the century, of their customs and integration into American life.   The five girls and
one little boy come quickly to life as their trials and tri-
umphs bring laughter and tears to the sympathetic reader.
They happily cavort through the chapter on Hanukkah sharing
gifts, games and family love.   The girls help their mother
prepare the traditional potato cakes or latkes.   The description of how the potatoes and onions are fried in the bubbling
hot oil would make any class eager to prepare its own feast
for Hanukkah.

Activities

      The activities which can result from a study of this
holiday are numerous.   The books can be read aloud in the
classroom and then become a basis for discussion of the
variety of customs and traditions surrounding the holiday season.   A Jewish child in the classroom might be asked to
share how his family celebrates this Festival of Lights.   A
menorah could be obtained (or made by the children) and the
custom of lighting the candles could be followed in the classroom if this is done with dignity and reverence and in appreciation of an ancient tradition.   Latkes can be made and
eaten.   Dreydls can be made and decorated correctly so that
children learn a bit of the Hebrew alphabet while enjoying
the fun games.   Don't be confused by the different spellings
of Hanhkah, Hanukkah, Chanuka, dreidel, dreydle, dredel,
dreidl, draydle, but simply stick with the spelling in the
book you are currently using as a resource.

FEBRUARY BIRTHDAYS

The birthday of Abraham Lincoln on February 12 is a legal holiday in 33 states. Lincoln was born February 12, 1809, the son of a poor farmer. He spent his early boyhood in Kentucky and was a self-taught man, having less than one year of formal schooling. He worked on his father's farm, as a rower on the Ohio River, as a clerk, as an officer in the militia, served in the Illinois Legislature, studied law, became a U.S. Representative, and finally became the 16th President of the United States. He was known for his stand on the abolition of slavery, one unified nation under one government, and for his honesty and integrity. He was assassinated in office.

The birthday of George Washington (February 22, 1732) is celebrated the third Monday in February. Son of a wealthy landowner, he spent most of his boyhood in Virginia and learned to manage a large plantation. He became a surveyor and a Colonel in the Army. He served as a delegate to the First Continental Congress, Commander of the Continental Army and First President of the United States. He believed in the freedom of the individual and the oneness of the American people.

Titles Suggested for Use	Suggested Grade Level
Bulla. Lincoln's Birthday	2-4
Bulla. Washington's Birthday	2-4
D'Aulaire. Abraham Lincoln	2-5
D'Aulaire. George Washington	2-5
Foster. Abraham Lincoln	3-6
Foster. George Washington	3-6
Judson. Abraham Lincoln, Friend of the People	4-6

Titles Suggested for Use	Suggested Grade Level
Judson. George Washington, Leader of the People	4-6
Monjo. Me and Willie and Pa	3-6
Norman. A Man Named Lincoln	K-3
Norman. A Man Named Washington	K-3
Steiner. George Washington--The Indian Influence	3-6

Most school libraries provide a wide variety of books which will help students to become better acquainted with two of their country's best known Presidents. If your school library does not have the specific titles reviewed here, which were selected for the most part because they have met the test of time, it will surely have a number of others which can stimulate the same kinds of learning and activities.

Bulla, Clyde Robert. Lincoln's Birthday. Illus. by Ernest Crichlow. Crowell, 1965. (2-4)
Bulla, Clyde Robert. Washington's Birthday. Illus. by Don Bolognese. Crowell, 1967. (2-4)
These are well-written accounts of the life stories of two famous Presidents appropriate for young independent readers. In addition to the traditional biographical material, these books include mention of monuments and tell how these presidential birthdays can be celebrated. In addition, both titles will read aloud well to primary grades.

D'Aulaire, Ingri and Edgar. Abraham Lincoln. Illus. by the authors. Doubleday, 1957. (2-5)
D'Aulaire, Ingri and Edgar. George Washington. Illus. by the authors. Doubleday, 1936. (2-5)
These master artists have created two beautiful books to enrich any classroom. The vivid and creative illustrations give a clear view into the times of the presidents' lives. The narrative is unbroken by imaginary dialogue (which often helps to liven up books for young children), but the illustrations alone, which grace every other page, will hold their attention.

Foster, Genevieve. Abraham Lincoln. Charles Scribner's,
    1950.   (3-6)
Foster, Genevieve. George Washington. Charles Scribner's,
    1949.   (3-6)
    These charming longer biographies hold an important
place in children's literature. They are geared for younger
readers than the author's outstanding George Washington's
World, and yet are authentic, conveying a unique understanding of the men and their times. A wide age-group can appreciate the drama and color of this writing. The books are
small, but brimming with information.

Judson, Clara Ingram. Abraham Lincoln, Friend of the
    People. Illus. by Robert Frankenberg. Follett, 1950.
    (4-6)
Judson, Clara Ingram. George Washington, Leader of the
    People. Illus. by Robert Frankenberg. Follett, 1951.
    (4-6)
    Here are two titles which have been long tested and
appreciated by those children who have discovered that biographies often make exciting reading. These two great
American Presidents fairly leap from the pages as they come
to life under the pen of a fine writer. The biography on
Lincoln has, in addition to the liberal pen and ink drawings,
fourteen reproductions of the Lincoln Dioramas of the Chi-
cago Historical Society. Appearing almost photographic,
they take the reader right into the Civil War era.

Monjo, F. N. Me and Willie and Pa--The Story of Abra-
    ham Lincoln and His Son, Tad. Illus. by Douglas Gors-
    line. Simon & Schuster, 1973. (3-6)
    This is the story of the Lincoln family's four years
in the White House (1861-1865). It is written as though their
son, Tad, had witnessed and recorded it. The humor of
Lincoln, the horror of war, the sadness and joy of growing
up in these times with a troubled family are all seen through
Tad's boyish eyes. No tragedy is glossed over, and there
was plenty in Lincoln's life! The numerous illustrations,
done to resemble steel engravings of the 1800s, will be
looked over at length if the book is left around a classroom
which has been enlightened about the life of this great-
hearted American and "unforgettable Pa."

Norman, Gertrude. A Man Named Lincoln. Illus. by

Joseph Cellini.   G. P. Putnam's, 1960.   (K-3)
Norman, Gertrude.   A Man Named Washington.   Illus. by
Joseph Cellini.   G. P. Putnam's, 1960.   (K-3)

In simple prose, the stories of these two Presidential
heroes are told for beginning readers.   The best-known
legends and events surrounding the two men from their child-
hoods to their deaths are related in comfortable language for
the youngest history buff.   Both books can be read aloud to
primary students.

Steiner, Stan.   George Washington: The Indian Influence.
Illus. by Fermin Rocker.   G. P. Putnam's, 1970.   (3-
6)

An interesting aspect of this President's life is treated
in big clear print and vivid line drawings.   The story of
Washington's rugged life as a child growing up in the wilder-
ness adds new dimension to this hero.   The fact that he was
not a scholar, that he ate with his fingers, danced with an
Indian war party and hunted bear, may give encouragement
to other non-scholars.   This is a book of high adventure.
Children will enjoy picturing George Washington at sixteen
years of age with his bright red hair, six-foot frame and
size thirteen shoes.   The story carries the reader through
the terrible suffering at Valley Forge where Washington's
background as a rough backwoodsman and the lessons learned
from the Indians helped his army to survive.   The index and
bibliography may prove helpful to young researchers.

Activities

1) Dialogue from any of these books or sections of the
books can be used in small skits within the classroom or
shared with other classrooms on the birthdays of these Presidents.

2) After hearing the biographies of these remarkable men
read aloud, children will be easily motivated to design a
birthday card for each or both of the former Presidents.
They can make a picture card, compose a poem or write
out an appropriate thought.   The room can be decorated with
these cards to celebrate these February birthdays.

3) After sharing biographies of these two men, ask students
which they would prefer as a father, as a President or as a
next-door-neighbor.   Be sure to give them time to share why
they feel as they do.

4) Make a list of the qualities which these men expressed which made them great. Are these qualities expressed in your classroom? The children might enjoy making charts listing the characteristics of each man; and each time one of these qualities or characteristics (honesty, integrity, etc.) is demonstrated by a student, a check could be made on the chart under that quality. At the end of a week, children can tally up the "Presidential Expectations" in the classroom. It could be an eye-opening experience for the class as a whole to see that, for example, they rate high on courage but need to work on tolerance.

5) During February your class might like to have a President for the Day. Before voting each day it might be helpful to talk about what made Washington and Lincoln good Presidents. Do the children care as much about their classroom as these men cared about their country? There is much food for thought and discussion in this type of activity.

6) A time-line of Presidents would be a helpful project to enable children to see just where Washington and Lincoln fit into their country's history.

7) A diorama of scenes from the lives of either of these men could be constructed from old shoe boxes and scraps of material. Each child could choose the scene he or she would like to create. When completed, let the children decide in which order they should be displayed. If there is disagreement concerning which event came first in a President's life, the biographies (which should be available in the classroom) will settle the question.

VALENTINE'S DAY

The history of Valentine's Day is not entirely clear, but the holiday is thought to have originated with the early Romans.   In ancient Rome a festival was held each year in February to honor the Roman hero, Lupercus, who killed many wolves.   During the festival young people chose partners for the year and exchanged gifts.   It is not certain which of the two St. Valentines the holiday is meant to honor. One was a Bishop of Rome who was beheaded in 270 A.D. during the persecution of the early Christians.   The other was a Roman priest who was imprisoned for performing marriages which had been forbidden by the Emperor Claudius. The first Valentine is credited to the Duke of Orleans, who in 1415 wrote such a message to his loved ones while imprisoned in the Tower of London.

Titles Suggested for Use	Suggested Grade Levels
Anglund. A Friend Is Someone Who Likes You	K-2
Barth. Hearts, Cupids and Red Roses	3-6
Bianco. The Valentine Party	K-2
Devlin. A Kiss for a Warthog	all ages
Hays. The Story of Valentine	4-6
Hopkins. I Loved Rose Ann	2-4
Lobel. Frog and Toad Are Friends	all ages
Lobel. Frog and Toad Together	K-3
Milhous. Appolonia's Valentine	1-4
Silverstein. The Giving Tree	all ages
Steig. Amos and Boris	K-3

Zolotow. Janey   K-2

Zolotow. My Friend John   K-2

Anglund, Joan Walsh. A Friend Is Someone Who Likes You.
    Illus. by the author. Harcourt, Brace & World, 1958.
    (K-2)
        This thoughtful little essay touches on a variety of
kinds of friendship, including wind, trees, animals, etc. It
also shows how to find friends by looking carefully, listening
intently and becoming aware of potential friendships. "Some
people have lots and lots of friends, some people have quite
a few friends, but everyone ... everyone in the whole world
has at least ONE friend. Where did you find yours?"

Activity

        Give each child in the class time to tell or write about
his or her best friend. The friend can be animate or inani-
mate, human or animal. Be sure the child tells WHY this
one is a friend. During Valentine week encourage each child
in the class to try making one new friend. Children might
eat lunch with someone different, give a valentine to someone
not thought of before, or play with someone new at recess.
It could be a real eye-opening "Everyone Is Special" week.

Barth, Edna. Hearts, Cupids and Red Roses. Illus. by
    Ursula Arndt. Seabury Press, 1974. (3-6)
        This blend of stories, poems and facts about Valen-
tine's Day can serve as a good source of information for
young researchers. Topics covered include the origin of the
holiday, old and new valentines, cupid, love birds, roses,
valentine lace, valentine colors and goodies. The book is indexed for ease of use and contains a bibliography for further
reading on the topic.

Activity

A VALENTINE PUZZLE

        Most Valentine cards contain rhyming verses of love
and friendship. Think of rhyming words which will help to
solve the puzzle below. The answer to each question is a
symbol of the holiday.

1. Think of a word that means dumb.   stupid

What Valentine symbol rhymes with this word?   CUPID

2. Think of a word that means begin. start
    What Valentine symbol rhymes with this word?   HEART

3. Think of a word that means run fast. race
    What Valentine symbol rhymes with this word?   LACE

4. Think of a word that means "letters put together."
    words
    What Valentine symbol rhymes with this word?   BIRDS

5. Think of a word that means units of time. hours
    What Valentine symbol rhymes with this word? FLOWERS

6. Think of a word that means fine. dandy
    What Valentine symbol rhymes with this word?   CANDY

Can you compose more Valentine puzzles similar to these?

Alternate Activity

        As children discover the history and meaning of the
many symbols of Valentine's Day, suggest a Valentine mobile
for the classroom which shows the many symbols of the holiday.   Simple mobiles can be made using cut paper objects
hung on large stiff soda straws with string or wire (see illustration).
        Build the mobile from the bottom.   Begin by making
several objects (at least six) which represent the holiday
from cut paper of appropriate color.   For a six-object mobile, five rods (straws) are needed--two short, two medium
and one long.   The short ones should be at least 4" in length.
Tie one of the finished objects to each end.   Find the balance point on the straw by holding it on your index finger until it hangs evenly and does not fall off.   Tie the holding
string at this point.   Take one of the medium length rods
and tie another of the objects to one end of it, and the string
which balances your shorter rod to the other end.   Do the
same with the other medium-length rod.   Find the balance
point for these sections and tie the string at that point.   You
now have two short mobiles which then tie to each end of
the long rod.   Find the balance point for this rod and put a
hold string at that point to hang the entire mobile in an area
that allows for free movement.
        Mobiles must balance.   To achieve this, both the
length of the string and its position on the rod or straw can

be adjusted. Lay the whole piece on a desk top as you work
and keep checking the total balance as you go along. Strong
black thread is a good string to use as it does not show and
gives the mobile a floating quality.

Bianco, Pamela. The Valentine Party. Illus. by the author.
     Lippincott, 1954. (K-2)
     A gentle story for the youngest, about a little girl who
thought that everyone was invited to a valentine party except
her. Instead of taking a nap as she was supposed to do, she
sneaked out of her bedroom and tried to follow the children
to the party. She lost them and came sadly home, only to
discover that the surprise party was for her. The girls in
frilly paper aprons and the boys in paper hats sang out,
"Happy Valentine Day, Cathy!"

Activity

     The illustrations in this little book are all framed
with lace doily edges. Have the children cut the lace edges
from doilies. Let them search through old magazines for
pictures they might cut out and frame with the lace edges
from the doilies. The resulting valentines can be used to
send or to decorate the classroom as pictures of "Our Favorite Things." The class might enjoy planning a surprise
party for the class next door or for the principal or custodian or school nurse.

Devlin, Wende and Harry. A Kiss for a Warthog. Illus. by
     Harry Devlin. Van Nostrand Reinhold Co., 1970. (all
     ages)
     "The Town of Oldwich and the Town of Quimby had
always been rivals." They competed in baking, baseball and
even in acquisitions for their local zoos. When the Quimby
Zoo obtained a warthog, the Town of Oldwich telephoned
Africa for an even better warthog. When "Allegra" arrived,
problems ensued, for she refused to leave the ship until she
was welcomed, just like everyone else, with a kiss. The
solution to the problem brings the two towns together in a
spirit of cooperation.

Activity

     This can serve as a delightful Valentine story and a
springboard for making special valentines for special people.

Two Lips are better than one

there are smiles...

and then

There are Smiles !

Love

ROOF

A class valentine might be made for the school nurse, custodian or principal for example, noting the ways in which the
class might cooperate more fully in helping these people to
do their jobs.

A valentine castle can help in the class's kindness
and good manners crusade. Have each student do a "Kindness is" or "Love is" tower from a sheet of paper 9" wide
by any height desired. This will become their "love tower."
It can be cut into a parapet top or have a cone-shaped roof.
Each tower should have at least one window which opens to
reveal a message of kindness or love or cheer (see illustration).

Hays, Wilma Pitchford.   The Story of Valentine.   Illus. by
    Leonard Weisgard.   Coward-McCann, 1956.   (4-6)
    The author has taken historical fact and has blended
it with fictional characters to re-create the story of St.
Valentine as it might have happened.   Ancient Rome was an
anti-Christian country.   Romans believed in twelve or more
gods, and those who professed belief in the one true God were
persecuted.   The priest, Valentine, was one of these and
was put into prison for his beliefs.   The Roman boys who
had visited him in his garden, and who had come to love and
respect him, felt the injustice of his imprisonment and were
able to communicate with him through written messages carried by Smoky, Valentine's tame pigeon.   One of the boys,
Octavian, takes on the perilous task of smuggling into the
prison Valentine's Book about the one God.   The jailer's
daughter, Julia, who is blind, is cured by Valentine and many
years later, when the Roman people had accepted belief in
one God, they decided to honor the good priest Valentine by
celebrating his birthday on February 14th of each year.

Activity

The importance of accuracy in recreating historical
scenes should be stressed to students.   Point out that the
author, Wilma Hays, had to do considerable research on the
topic of Ancient Rome in order to portray the people and
places of that time accurately.   Ask students if they recall
any of the details which clearly indicate that the time of the
story is ancient Rome and not present-day Rome.   (Words
recalled might be: charioteer, Emperor, quill, gladiator,
rolled book, Forum, Saturnalia, and toga.)   Divide the class
into small groups.   Let each group select a word or term
from the story about which they would like to know more.

Each group should be allowed time in the school library to
do research on the word or term.   When all groups have located and compiled their information their findings should be
shared with the class.   If interest in this time period is running high, a table model of a Roman town can be created.
One group might accept responsibility for finding out what the
homes looked like and for constructing homes from construction paper, cardboard or popsicle sticks.   Another group can
be responsible for types of transportation, another for clothing, and perhaps another for the types of crops or plants
which were native to the area.

Hopkins, Lee Bennett.   I Loved Rose Ann.   Illus. by Ingrid
     Fetz.   Alfred A. Knopf, 1976.   (2-4)
          As Lee Hopkins tells the stories of Harry Hooper and
Rose Ann, it becomes obvious that there are, indeed, two
sides to every story! Each story, told in the first person,
relates similar incidents but from the point of view of the
speaker.   From Harry's point of view, Rose Ann is mean
when she rejects both his flower and his two valentines.
From Rose Ann's viewpoint, Harry is really pretty nice but
she is not quite ready to turn a friendship into a love affair.

Activity

          Discuss with students the importance of investigating
both sides of an issue before drawing conclusions.   Recall
some familiar fairy tales (Snow White, Little Red Riding
Hood).   Ask students to think of the story from the point of
view of the "bad guy" (the queen in Snow White; the wolf in
Little Red Riding Hood).   Can any student give a good reason why the queen (or the wolf) acted as she did?   Groups
of students should be challenged to choose an old tale and retell it from the point of view of the antagonist (the bad guy)
rather than the protagonist.   Story boards could be made of
the tales and write-on filmstrips produced.   Each group
should show its filmstrip to the class, accompanied by live
or recorded narration of the script.

Lobel, Arnold.   Frog and Toad Are Friends.   Illus. by the
     author.   Harper & Row, 1970.   (all ages)
          This is a story of friendship between two delightful
characters.   Five short chapters describe different adven-
tures and differing aspects of friendship.   Easy vocabulary
but fresh and original ideas tell about situations familiar to

all. Toad doesn't want to get out of bed. Frog doesn't feel
well. Toad loses a button off his jacket. Toad is embar-
rassed and looks funny in his bathing suit, and everybody
knows how he feels when he doesn't get any mail. A charming book to use around Valentine's Day to show children the
real meaning of affection among friends.

Activity

        Perfect little skits can be constructed from these
simple, yet funny stories. Frog and toad faces can be created on brown paper bags to be worn for presentations.
Small finger puppets can be made in minutes to portray the
characters. Hand puppets or stick puppets can be used over
and over again. When these first stories are exhausted, the
sequel, Frog and Toad Together, has five new stories which
are every bit as much fun to use. Children can memorize
the dialogues, or good readers can read them aloud while
other children pantomime in puppet or in person.

Lobel, Arnold. Frog and Toad Together. Illus. by the au-
     thor. Harper & Row, 1971. (K-3)
        In these five gentle stories of friendship, frog and
toad once again share a variety of experiences, each one
touched with humor. When toad loses his list of things to
do, frog helps him remember. When toad's seeds won't
grow, frog reassures him. The two friends share everything
from cookies to scary experiences, and even in his dreams
toad discovers that fame is nothing compared to having a
good friend.

Activity

        These short but delightful stories are perfect for dra-
matic play. Children working in pairs can select one story
from this book or any of the other "Frog and Toad" books
by Lobel and read their favorite story together until they
are quite familiar with it. One member of the pair can describe the setting of the story for the class (toad's bedroom? the edge of the woods? etc.) and use chairs to serve
as trees or toad's bed or whatever is needed. Lines should
not be memorized but the action told in the students own
words. Be sure students are aware that Frog and Toad always treat each other with kindness and are always very careful with each other's feelings.

Milhous, Katherine. <u>Appolonia's Valentine.</u> Illus. by the
     author. Scribner's, 1954. (1-4)
          Appolonia and Dan attended a one-room Pennsylvania
Dutch schoolhouse. When Appolonia could not make a valentine which satisfied her, she sold eggs at the market until
she had enough money to buy a paintbox. After many at-
tempts she finally painted a valentine which pleased her, and
sent it to a pen-pal in France. He responded with cut-outs
and a heart-warming letter. Pennsylvania Dutch designs
decorate the pages and offer ideas from the Old World to
share in Valentine greetings.

Activity

     Children may want to try their hands at pin pricking
or cut-outs to create valentines. Talk with the class about
people who might not be remembered at Valentine's Day.
Explore the possibility in your community of sharing valentines with the residents of a senior citizens' home or a nursing home. Other possibilities include patients in a children's
hospital or a state hospital for the mentally retarded.

Silverstein, Shel. <u>The Giving Tree.</u> Illus. by the author.
     Harper & Row, 1964. (all ages)
          "Once there was a tree ... and she loved a little
boy." So begins a story of unforgettable perception, beautifully written and illustrated. Every day the boy would come
to the tree to eat her apples, swing from her branches, or
slide down her trunk ... and the tree was happy. But as
the boy grew older he began to want more from the tree, and
the tree gave and gave and gave. This is a tender story,
touched with sadness, aglow with consolation. Shel Silverstein has created a moving parable for readers of all ages
that offers an affecting interpretation of the gift of giving and
a serene acceptance of another's capacity to love in return.
(Publisher's note)

Activity

     This is a most appropriate story for use around Valen-
tine's Day, for it defines rather clearly the concept that real
love means giving completely of one's self. Discuss with the
class the ways in which others (mother, father, friends) give
of themselves to us and the ways in which we give of our-
selves to others. As children begin to see the concept of
love as giving of one's self, ask them to try writing defini-

tions of love.   Large letters on the bulletin board might spell
out LOVE IS ... with the students' definitions and/or illustrations surrounding it.

Steig, William.   Amos and Boris.   Illus. by the author.
     Farrar, Straus and Girous, 1971.   (K-3)
     This is a delightful story of friendship between a very
large whale and a very small mouse.   Learning to love and
trust one another, they have a reciprocal opportunity to save
each other's lives.

Activity

     With the help of the school librarian collect as many
books as possible on friendship for the classroom reading
table.   (Other possibilities are Arnold Lobel's Frog and Toad
series, James Marshall's George and Marsha, Joan Walsh
Anglund's A Friend Is Someone Who Likes You, Lee Bennett
Hopkins' I Loved Rose Ann, and Charlotte Zolotow's My
Friend John.)   Encourage the children to notice, as they
browse through this "friendship collection," the different kinds
of friendship.   Some friendships develop because we are so
much alike, some because we are a little different, and others because we are totally different!   Thinking of the value
of different kinds of friendships can lead to valuable classroom discussions about love and caring for each other.   "We
don't have to be alike to be friends" is the message in these
books, but sometimes that is fun too!

Zolotow, Charlotte.   Janey.   Illus. by Ronald Himler.   Harp-
     er and Row, 1973.   (K-2)
     What does it mean when a friend moves away?   Janey's
friend remembers all of the simple things they did together,
like touching wet leaves, skipping rocks, telephone calls, exchanging presents, listening to the wind or just sitting together quietly.   This perceptive story will touch all children
who have had a friend move away or who have had to move
themselves.

Zolotow, Charlotte.   My Friend John.   Illus. by Ben Shecter.
     Harper & Row, 1968.   (K-2)
     Good friends know everything about each other, like
secret places and who needs a night light and who is best at
spelling (or fighting).   They know each other's likes, dis-

likes and fears, and are always ready to help when they can.
The hero of this story tells of his friend John, saying, "I
know who he really likes and he knows about Mary, too!"
No greater evidence of friendship can be found than this!

Activity

Decorate the classroom with illustrated friendship
lists for Valentine's Day. Start the children thinking about
friendship with these two delightful books. Write on the
chalkboard these words: "A good friend is someone who ... "
Ask the class for suggestions as to how this sentence might
be completed. Ask the children individually to write three
sentences which begin this way. Each child should then
choose the sentence he has written which he thinks best de-
scribes what friendship is. His definition can be illustrated
as a part of a friendship bulletin board.

ST. PATRICK'S DAY

St. Patrick's Day, March 17th, is celebrated as a national holiday in Ireland and is also a popular holiday with Irish-Americans in the United States. The day honors the Patron Saint of Ireland who, at the age of 16, was captured and sold into slavery in Ireland but escaped six years later and returned to his home in England. In the year 432 he returned to Ireland to battle the powerful Druids (Irish priests) in an attempt to bring the Christian belief to this pagan land. He built hundreds of churches and baptized thousands of people. Of the many legends told about him, perhaps the most popular is of his driving the snakes of Ireland into the Irish sea by beating on his drum.

Suggested Titles for Use	Suggested Grade Level
Danaher. Folktales of the Irish Countryside	4-6
Dolch. Irish Stories	1-4
Green. Philip and the Pooka	4-6
Holland. From Famine to Fame	3-6
Jagendorf. Ghostly Folktales	5-6
Johnson. The Irish in America	4-6
MacMahon. Patsy-O and His Wonderful Pets	1-3
Payne. The Leprechaun of Bayou Luce	2-4
Shura. A Shoefull of Shamrock	all ages

Danaher, Kevin. Folktales of the Irish Countryside. Illus. by Harold Berson. David White, 1970. (4-6)
     This is a collection of fourteen Irish tales which were compiled by the author who heard them as a child in County

Limerick in Ireland. "Shaped by the lyric lilt of native
speech, these tales are filled with the mystery and adventure of a land of lonely country roads and isolated farms,
humble cottages and lordly castles, rolling fields and tract-
less bogs. They tell of giants and ghosts, of queer happen-
ings and wondrous deeds, of fairies and witches, and of fools
and kings." (Publisher's note.) This is, indeed, a varied
collection of tales which should keep young listeners begging
for more when the last tale has been told.

Activity

Preceding the stories in the book is a glossary of
Irish terms. What fun it would be for students to learn and
to be able to use some of the terms on St. Patrick's Day!
Duplicate the following Irish terms for students to match with
their English translation. Who can remember the story from
which the terms came? Students may want to illustrate a
chart of Irish words for the bulletin board.

amadan (foolish person)	plannc (chunk)
a mhaoineach (my dear)	puck goat (billy goat)
bodhran (drum)	sidle gaoithe (whirlwind)
brosna (bundle of sticks)	sopog (piece of straw or hay)
croitin (hut)	stirabout (porridge)
giobals (rags)	tuppence (two pennies)
Ochon O (Oh, woe!)	Ulagon O (Oh, alas!)

Alternate Activity

Some students may enjoy serving as word detectives;
as other Irish folktales are read, or as they find other tales
in the school or public library, these words and their mean-
ings can be added to the chart.

When the collection of Irish words has grown to fifty
or more, children can make illustrated dictionaries of Irish
words and phrases. Those children who show an interest in
different types of lettering (calligraphy) will enjoy doing large
posters of Irish words and phrases, each word or phrase let-
tered in a different style and running in all directions on the
poster. Through such an activity students will come to realize that lettering itself can be an art form.

Dolch, Edward W. and Marguerite. Irish Stories. Illus.
    by Carmen Mowry. Garrard, 1958. (1-4)
    This is a collection of "read it yourself" tales that

will be enjoyed by the advanced first grade reader, second
and third grade readers, and reluctant fourth grade readers.
There are stories of witches, fairies, leprechauns and
dwarfs, as well as stories of humor and suspense. In the
first story, "A Basket of Eggs," an old woman spies a leprechaun as she is taking her eggs to market. She catches him
and refuses to let him go until he shows her his pot of gold.
Not only does she NOT get the pot of gold but she loses all
her eggs as well, as she is outsmarted by the little fellow.
But she is not totally miserable, for hasn't the leprechaun
told her that she was "a beautiful woman!"

Activity

The playground is just the place for a St. Patrick's
Day game. Try a "Potato Basket Relay" (safer than an "Egg
Basket Relay!"). Explain that potatoes are a very important
crop in Ireland and that the old woman might well have been
taking a sack of potatoes to market instead of a sack of eggs.
Divide the children into teams. Put a pile of potatoes in
front of each team and a basket about 20 feet or more away
from each team. On a signal, the first team member on
each team picks up a potato, runs and puts it in the basket,
then runs to tag the next team member, who repeats the action. The team which gets all the potatoes in the basket
first wins.

Green, Kathleen. Philip and the Pooka. Illus. by Victoria
    de Larrea. Lippincott, 1966. (4-6)
    "These are stories about the magic folk who will leap
into your heart and stay forever. You will meet Pooka, the
fairy horse, the Wise Woman (she tried so hard to tidy her
mind), Fergus Og, the lord of the fairies, the Ugly Person
(who wasn't so bad), the Fairy Dancers, the Lochrie-men
(they were a bit taller than Leprechauns), Barney O'Dowd's
Dragon, and many more of the alert, witty, and lovable inhabitants of the magical glens of Ireland. Ride the Pooka
with us up the lane to the Fairy Fort." (Publisher's note.)

Activity

No St. Patrick's Day celebration would be complete
without the sharing of one or more of these delightful Irish
tales. Along with the sharing of tales which are filled with
stories of magic people, shamrocks, the wearing of the
green, leprechauns and the blarney stone, children will have

fun with some simple quizzes on St. Patrick's Day symbols.
Try this one on "The Wearing of the Green."

1. The moon is made of (green cheese)

2. A northern country (Greenland)

3. A kind of money (greenback)

4. A vegetable (green bean)

5. Foliage or plants (greenery)

6. Jealous (greeneyed)

7. A kind of plum (greengage)

8. A glass enclosure for growing plants (greenhouse)

9. Ability to grow plants (green thumb)

10. Basis of standard time (Greenwich)

Add others for friends to puzzle over!

1. To cover a hole (PATch)

2. Kind of quilt (PATchwork)

3. Kind of leather (PATent)

4. A marked area to follow (PATh)

5. One who attends or supports an institution (PATron)

6. Sound of little feet (PATter)

7. Used in making clothing (PATtern)

8. Shape of a hamburger (PATty)

9. Attached to the side or rear of a house (PATio)

10. A fatherly pat (PATernal)

Explore your dictionary to find other PATS for St. Patrick's
Day!

Holland, Ruth. From Famine to Fame. Illus. by Charles
     Waterhouse. Grosset & Dunlap, 1967. (3-6)
         This is an easy to read true account of the Irish in
America. Beginning with a description of the Great Famine
in Ireland in the mid 1800s, the author tells in an interesting
way the reasons for the Irish immigration to the United
States, including background information of the 700 years of

domination of the Irish by the English.   The hardships of the
journey and the prejudice met by the immigrants once they
reached the shores of the New World are vividly described.
But throughout the text runs the theme of the Irish courage
and determination which helped these people to achieve fame
in their chosen land.   A brief discussion of famous Irish-
Americans is included.

Activity

        Whether the book is read aloud to the class or in-
dividual students, use the book as a source of information
on the Irish in America, the following puzzle will serve as
a check on the students' comprehension of what has been
read.

1.	F - - - - -	7.	- - T - - - -
2.	- A - - - - - - - - - -	8.	- O - - - - -
3.	- M - - - - - - - -	9.	F - - -
4.	I - - - - -	10.	- - - A - - -
5.	- - - N - - - - - - - - -	11.	M - - - - - - - - -
6.	E - - - - - - - - - -	12.	E - - - - - -

Directions

        Complete the book title puzzle above by answering the
following questions:

1.   Why many Irish came to America in the mid-1800s.

2.   The Patron Saint of Ireland.

3.   People who come to live in a new land.

4.   The land form of Ireland.

5.   Price of a boat ticket to America in 1850.

6.   Nickname for Ireland.

7.   Religion of many Irish immigrants.

8.   A major crop of Ireland.

9.   The ocean voyage of America took _____ weeks.

10.   He created San Francisco's first system of street lights.

11.   Famous Irish-American woman, known as "Unsinkable."

12.   Until 1922 Ireland was ruled by _____.

Jagendorf, M. A.   Ghostly Folktales.   Illus. by Oscar Lieb-
       man.   Silver Burdett, 1968.   (5-6)
       The first in this truly scary collection of folktales
from all over the world is from Ireland.   In "The Coffinmaker's Ghost Party," a coffinmaker attends a wake for a
deceased friend.   While there, he is urged to consider marriage with one of several unattached females.   As his anger
grows at this invasion of his privacy, he states that he would
rather entertain all of the dead friends for whom he had made
coffins than the woman who had irritated him so.   When he
reaches his home he finds that his invitation to the dead has
been accepted and that his house is filled with truly horrify-
ing specters who proceed to make him change his mind concerning the desirability of inviting ghosts to a party!

Activity

       In Ireland, one who is a good story teller is said to
have kissed the "Blarney Stone."   Have the children make
their own Blarney Stones (which can be used as table center-
pieces at home on St. Patrick's Day).   Needed is a stone
about five to seven inches long and three to five inches wide
and high.   Also needed is a box lid at least nine by twelve
inches (or larger), green construction paper, pipe cleaners
and modeling clay.   Two empty spools of thread glued near
the center of the underside of the box lid will help to support
the weight of the stone.
       Cover the lid with green construction paper or crepe
paper.   Glue the stone in the center of the lid.   Cut out
shamrock patterns of several sizes and blue or tape each to
one end of a pipe cleaner.   Put the other end of the cleaner
through a small hole made in the lid.   Shamrocks can be
placed in any position around the stone.   Various sizes of
shamrocks will make a more attractive centerpiece.   Fashion
snakes from the modeling clay and place them on the lid near
the stone.   This makes a basic centerpiece.   Students who
are especially creative may want to shape small figures from
the pipe cleaners and dress them appropriately in crepe paper
costumes.
       The class may want to consider inviting another class
to a St. Patrick's Day Party.   Smaller versions of the Blarney
Stone (perhaps a small stone wrapped in green crepe paper
and tied with a green or white ribbon, under which has been

placed a paper shamrock) can be made as party favors for
the guests.   Irish songs can be sung ("The Wearing of the
Green" and "When Irish Eyes Are Smiling"); one student might
give a brief history of the holiday; blindfolded players can try
pinning a paper shamrock on Ireland (found on a large map of
Europe pinned to the bulletin board); teams of players can
take part in a Kiss the Blarney Stone Relay.   In this game
a stone is placed about 30 feet from the leader of each team.
At a given signal, the team leader races for the stone, kisses
it and races back to touch the next player in line, and so on
until one team finishes first.

If hand-cranked ice cream freezers are brought to
school, green ice cream can be made for everyone by adding
a bit of green food coloring to the ice cream mix.   (Use
your favorite recipe.)   One freezer-full will provide a modest
serving for 20 children.

Johnson, James E.   The Irish in America.   Illus. with pho-
    tographs.   Lerner Publications, 1967.   (4-6)
        This book is an excellent source of information about
the Irish people who came to America to make their fortunes.
The hardships of the Great Famine of the 1800s are described,
the reasons for the decision of many to make the dangerous
voyage and the voyage itself are detailed.   The difficult life
of the immigrant in the United States and his struggle to create a better life for himself and his children are described,
as well as the role of the Irish in the Civil War.   The book
is an excellent source of information about the contributions
in many fields of endeavor which have been made by Irish
Americans.   Included are Irish literary figures, people in
music, sports, the Church, architecture, the military, business and politics.

Activity

The contributions of Irish Americans to the United
States are many and varied.   How appropriate it would be
on St. Patrick's Day to share information about famous Irish
Americans.   Ask for volunteers (a few days before the holiday) to seek information about one of the following people and
to be prepared to share their information with the class on
St. Patrick's Day.

Eugene O'Neill   Victor Herbert   Fred Allen
F. Scott Fitzgerald   Bing Crosby   Ed Sullivan

John O'Hara	Jackie Gleason	John L. Sullivan
John McCormack	Grace Kelly	Jack Dempsey
George M. Cohan	Helen Hayes	Ben Hogan
John F. Kennedy	Tom Dooley	Louis Sullivan
Edward M. Kennedy	Richard Daley	Colin P. Kelly

MacMahon, Bryan. Patsy-O and His Wonderful Pets. Illus.
    by Imero Gobbato. E. P. Dutton, 1970. (1-3)
        Patsy-O lived with his mother, his sister and his five
pets--a cricket, a cat, a cock, a donkey and a dog--and lived
each day happily until one day the family savings were gone
and Patsy-O set off to make his fortune. He promised to
return home by Christmas Eve. Taking his dead father's car-
pentry tools, the boy became a successful carpenter, saved
his money, and, as Christmas Eve neared, prepared for the
journey home. An encounter with a band of smugglers de-
lays his journey and he is thrown into the sea in a barrel;
but as luck will have it, the barrel floats near his own home-
land and he is rescued by his wonderful pets! This is a tale
which may take more than one reading time to tell, but the
primary children should take Patsy-O to their hearts and enjoy every word.

Activity.

     With the help of the art teacher or of one or more
upper grade students, make an outline drawing of each of
Patsy-O's pets on a separate ditto master. After copies are
run they can be cut up (jigsaw puzzle fashion) and placed in
envelopes. When the story is completed, give each child an
envelope, and let him put the animals back together again.
As each child discovers the animal made by his puzzle, he
might make up a bit of dialogue to tell what the animal might
have said to welcome Patsy-O home. (Puzzles can be glued
together on another sheet of paper and colored if desired.)

Payne, Joan. The Leprechaun of Bayou Luce. Illus. by
    the author. Hastings House, 1957. (2-4)
        For action lovers this story of a displaced leprechaun
can't be beaten! Josh Turnipseed, a Mississippi bayou boy,
meets a strange little man on the bayou one day and becomes
involved in the little man's scheme to recover the pot of gold
that had been stolen from him by the pirate "hants." Josh
agrees to help in exchange for a piece of gold to buy his baby
sister some shoes, but getting rid of "hants" proves to be no

easy task. With the help of an Indian chief, and some magic powers that Josh is unaware he possesses, the gold is recovered but not before the reader has some hair-raising moments!

Activity

Read the story aloud to page 48 (end of first paragraph). At this point in the story things look pretty hopeless. Josh, Chief Long James Panther and the leprechaun, as well as Dunc, the dog, are being hotly pursued by the pirates. Neither arrows nor bullets nor Dunc's teeth had any effect on the pirate ghosts. Josh has fallen and the chest of gold has been dropped. Ask students what possible solutions they think the author may come up with to end the story. Accept as many solutions as are given. Complete the story and see whether or not the children like the author's ending best or prefer one of their own.

Shura, Mary Francis. A Shoefull of Shamrock. Illus. by
    N. M. Bodecker. (all ages)
    If time permits the sharing of only one story to celebrate St. Patrick's Day, this heartwarming tale would be a first choice! David O'Sullivan lives with his immigrant parents and baby sister in New York City at the turn of the century. What the family lacks in material possessions they make up in love. The finding of a pouch of gold and its return to a strange little man leads to a promise which is made to Davy. As the little man gives the boy a strange green plant he says, "one day, the very streets of this town will look green like Ireland herself. And on that day if you've a leaf of this plant on you, and the first robin of your spring has been fed, you'll get your wish ... your inside secret wish ...." Davy's love for his family and his belief in the magic of the shamrock does bring his dearest wish, but in a realistic rather than magical way.

Activity

If at all possible, before the holiday visit a local florist and purchase a small live shamrock plant. Place it in a prominent spot in the classroom but do not tell the children what it is. After reading the story aloud, ask the class if they NOW know what kind of plant has been growing in their room. Older children may want to find out more about the plant, including how to care for it, where it is found

naturally and the folklore associated with it.   You can be
sure it will be the best-cared-for plant in the entire school
for the rest of the school year!

    After talking about the plant with younger children,
distribute green construction paper shamrocks which have
been prepared ahead of time.   Ask the children if they can
think of anyone they know (a friend, a member of the family)
who might have a wish that they could help make come true.
For example, has mother ever said, "I wish you would hang
up your clothes when you come home after school"?   Let
each child think of the wish of another that he or she could
help to bring true.   Tell the children to hide their shamrock
among the belongings of this person (in mother's kitchen
drawer, in a friend's lunch box or coat pocket).   Then, do
whatever is necessary to help the wish come true ... hang
up your clothes, dry the dishes without complaining, take out
the trash without being told, etc.   The real magic of the
shamrock comes in NOT telling the recipient what will happen when he or she receives it.   Perhaps when they see their
wishes come true they will believe in the magic of the shamrock, too!

EASTER (SPRING)

Background Information

The celebration of Easter is the celebration by Christians of eternal life as found in the resurrection of Jesus Christ. The date varies, being the first Sunday after the vernal equinox. The holiday is probably named after Eostre, the Goddess of Spring. The celebration of the coming of spring dates back to the ancient Egyptians, Romans and Mesopotamians. The egg as a symbol of life and the dying of eggs in the spring were prevalent ideas and practices in ancient Egypt, Rome, Greece and Persia.

The lamb as a symbol of Easter is taken from the Jewish celebration of Passover where the lamb was sacrificed. Christians view the sacrifice of the lamb as symbolic of the sacrifice Jesus made for man. The cross symbolizes the crucifixion of Christ and the Easter lily the new life which comes forth each spring.

Suggested Titles for Use	Suggested Grade Level
Andersen. The Ugly Duckling	all ages
Balian. Humbug Rabbit	K-2
Brown. The Runaway Bunny	K-2
Delton. Rabbit Finds a Way	K-3
Flora. Little Hatchy Hen	2-4
Francoise. Jeanne Marie Counts Her Sheep	K-1
Francoise. Springtime for Jeanne Marie	K-1
Freschet. The Old Bullfrog	all ages
Gay. The Nicest Time of the Year	K-2

Gay. Small One	K-2
Georgiou. The Nest	K-2
Hader. Two Is Company, Three's a Crowd	2-4
Heyward. The Country Bunny and the Little Gold Shoes	K-3
Hoban. Egg Thoughts and Other Frances Songs	all ages
House. The Lonesome Egg	1-4
Hutchins. Rosie's Walk	all ages
Hutchins. The Wind Blew	all ages
Ipcar. The Wonderful Egg	1-3
Keats. Jennie's Hat	K-2
Kuskin. The Bear Who Saw the Spring	K-2
Lund. Attic of the Wind	all ages
McCloskey. Make Way for Ducklings	K-2
Martin. I Paint the Joy of a Flower	all ages
Miles. Rabbit Garden	1-3
Milhous. The Egg Tree	all ages
Patterson. /Barth. Easter. /Lilies, Rabbits, Etc.	all ages
Politi. Song of the Swallows	all ages
Potter. The Tale of Peter Rabbit	K-2
Stone. The Last Free Bird	all ages
Thayer. The Horse with the Easter Bonnet	K-3
Tresselt. The World in the Candy Egg	all ages
Williams. The Velveteen Rabbit	all ages
Young. Miss Suzy's Easter Surprise	K-3

Additional Activity

Spring Birthdays	all ages

Andersen, Hans Christian. The Ugly Duckling. Illus. by
   Adrienne Adams. Scribner's, 1965. (all ages)

The Ugly Duckling
by Hans Christian Andersen

Cut the pictures apart. Put
them in order as they are
found in the story. Tell the
story in your own words.

This is the classic tale of the ugly duckling who is rejected by all of the other farm creatures because he does not look anything like the rest of mother duck's brood. His rejection leads him to escape out into the world where much pain and sorrow await him. In time, however, the "duckling" matures and one beautiful day looks at its reflection in a lake and sees not an ugly duckling, but a beautiful swan.

Activity--Primary

Even very young children can be led to grasp the idea that there is something beautiful in each one of us and we have only to look for it to find it. Prepare a ditto master of illustrations similar to those shown here. Ask the children to color the pictures and then to cut them apart. Can each child place the pictures in order on his desk in the order each event happened in the story? Some children may want to retell the story in their own words.

Activity--Intermediate

This story presents a wonderful opportunity for presenting to children the music for the Tchaikovsky's Swan Lake ballet. Tell the children the story of the ballet before playing the music. Ask them if there are moments in the music which might reflect scenes from The Ugly Duckling as well. Many can be found!

Balian, Lorna. Humbug Rabbit. Illus. by the author.
    Abingdon Press, 1974. (K-2)
    Each page in the book reveals the continuing action in two separate stories which at the end become one. Granny has invited her grandchildren for Easter but has a hard time finding where her hen has hidden the eggs. When she does find them she colors them and hides them in readiness for the children's visit. Meanwhile, in their burrow just beneath Granny's front yard, the little bunnies pester their father about when he is going to lay the Easter eggs (for they believe he is the Easter bunny). "Nonsense," says father, "rabbits do not lay eggs!" When Easter morning arrives, the children cannot find a single egg (for the cat has pushed them all down the rabbit holes during the night), but imagine the surprise of the baby bunnies to see the colored eggs in their burrow and the surprise of both the bunnies and the children when the eggs hatch and the chicks make their way out of the rabbit holes. The children and bunnies

play with the chicks, mother rabbit spreads colored egg
shells all over the floor, and father rabbit is left wondering
if the Easter bunny is really a humbug after all.

Activity

The sharing of this delightful story is an activity in
itself; however, it also provides an opportunity for discussion
about baby chicks as pets.   In this story the chicks remain
on the farm, but often children do receive chicks for Easter
and the undesirability of this practice can be pointed out, especially if an officer of the local humane society can be invited to speak to the class about "Easter pets."

Brown, Margaret Wise.   The Runaway Bunny.   Illus. by
    Clement Hurd.   Harper & Row, 1942.   (K-2)
    Little bunny's imagination knows no bounds as he de-
cides to run away from home.   He dreams up all kinds of
ways that mother can never find him, becoming a fish, a
mountain climber, a crocus, a bird and a sailboat, but mother always finds the flaw in his dreams.   If, for example, little bunny becomes a sailboat, then mother tells him that she
will become the wind and blow the boat wherever she wants
it to go.   The story comes full circle as, at the end, little
bunny finds himself snuggled happily in mother's arms.

Activity

The story introduces the idea of how things go together.   The children might cite such examples as the garden
and the gardener, the sailboat and the wind, etc.   Students
might enjoy playing "If I Were..." to reinforce the concepts
in the story.   One child begins with an "If I were..."--for
example, "If I were a cat...."   He calls on another student
to finish the sentence.   One answer might be "I would bring
you a big bowl of thick cream."   The child who completes
the sentence starts with a new "If I were" and calls on another student to complete it.   Encourage imaginative thought
and descriptive words.

Delton, Judy.   Rabbit Finds a Way.   Illus. by Joe Lasker.
    Crown, 1975.   (K-3)
    Rabbit is on his way to bear's house, for every Satur-
day morning Bear makes carrot cake.   On the way he turns
down offers of food from his other forest friends, only to find

that bear has overslept on this particular morning and has
not baked a cake. As rabbit heads home he finds that all
of the previously offered treats have been eaten and any treat
he will have on this day he will have to make himself. A
telephone call to bear for the recipe for carrot cake solves
the problem.

Activity

        Ask for one or more volunteers to visit the school li-
brary to locate a recipe for carrot cake. The librarian
should be forewarned concerning the young researchers' visit,
so that immediate help can be forthcoming. As children are
led to the 600 section of the library they might be allowed
time to browse through the books to locate those on food and
cooking. Help may be needed in using the index of a cook-
book to locate a particular recipe. The recipe can be written on the chalkboard for all the children to see. A vote can
be taken to see whether or not the children think that these
ingredients would make a cake which would be good to eat.
If a willing mother is available, perhaps small cupcakes
could be made at home (using the recipe) and brought to
school for the children to enjoy. Children will be delighted
to discover that carrot cake is really very good!

Flora, James. Little Hatchy Hen. Illus. by the author.
        Harcourt, Brace and World, 1969. (2-4)
        A hilarious story of a hen who could hatch anything
from pianos to barns. Her warm attention could create 200
feet of fire hose from a box of spaghetti. It was inevitable
that a crook would discover her prowess and exploit her
talents for his own ends. Big Bruno captured Hatchy Hen
and forced her to produce at his command. When he discovered that she could hatch hair on a bald man's head from
a toothbrush, he hit pay dirt. But exhaustion finally set in
and Hatchy Hen fell asleep on the job, and produced a head
covered with feathers. The furious customer gave Hatchy an
idea. She would hatch everything wrong and thus get sent
back to the farm. Her dream finally came true when she
hatched a dinosaur egg and the resulting monster adopted her
as his mother and rescued her. Back on the farm the dinosaur helped to hatch the 739 baby chicks waiting for Hatchy.
A really TALL tale!

Activity

        Have a contest in your classroom to see who can write

the funniest tall tale which involves the springtime hatching
of eggs. Writers can either work in small groups or individually. It will take really creative thinking to outdo James
Flora!

Francoise.   Jeanne Marie Counts Her Sheep.   Illus. by the
     author.   Scribners, 1951.   (K-1)
     This delightful counting book for the very youngest
tells of Jeanne Marie and her lamb, Patapon.   Jeanne Marie
speculates about what she can buy if Patapon has one little
lamb, or two or three, etc.   Patapon insists that all of the
things she dreams of are not needed, for nature supplies all
needs of its creatures.   At the end of the story Patapon does
have one little lamb, which eventually gives just enough wool
for one small pair of socks!

Activity

     If possible, reproduce on a ditto master a drawing
similar to the one shown here.   In coloring the picture by
the number of each color as given (1, red; 2, blue; 3, green;
4, yellow; 5, pink; 6, white) children will quickly demonstrate
their skills in number and color identification.   Check each
child's picture carefully and be prepared to give additional
help to students who show difficulty with either concept.
     When pictures have been completed, divide the class
into pairs.   Let each pair develop a short conversation between Jeanne Marie and Patapon (it does not have to be from
the book) and do the dialogue for the class as they show their
finished pictures.

Francoise.   Springtime for Jeanne Marie.   Illus. by the au-
     thor.   Scribners, 1955.   (K-1)
     "Jeanne Marie, Patapon, Madelon, we are three. "   In
this charming story the little French girl, Jeanne-Marie,
loses her little white duck, Madelon, and sets out, accompanied by Patapon, the lamb, to find her lost friend.   On her
search she meets the postman, the children at school, a fisherman and a little boy in a boat.   When Jeanne Marie reaches
a point of despair, her new friend takes her to his house,
where he offers her one of his five ducks.   However, the five
ducks have suddenly become six--the naughty Madelon is found
--and Jeanne Marie discovers that she has found something
else as well ... a new friend!

Jeanne-Marie Counts her Sheep
by Francoise

Color by Numbers

Color by number. Tell a friend what is happening in the story.

1 - Red	3 - Green	5 - Pink
2 - Blue	4 - Yellow	6 - White

Springtime for Jeanne-Marie by Francoise

Color the picture ... remember the colors from the book.
Cut the picture on the heavy black lines. Color and cut out
Madelon and Patapon. Fold the strips at the bottom of the
picture on the dotted lines (like a fan). Paste the animals
to the end of the folded strips for a moving, wiggling picture.

3-D Picture

Activity

Prepare a ditto master similar to the illustration
shown here.   Distribute copies to each child.   Ask the children to color the picture ... remember the colors from the
book.   Color and cut out Madelon and Patapon.   Cut as directed and fold the strips at the bottom of the picture on the
dotted lines (like a fan).   Paste the animals to the end of
the folded strips for a moving, wiggling picture.

Freschet, Berniece.   The Old Bullfrog.   Illus. by Roger
    Duvoisin.   Charles Scribner's Sons, 1968.   (all ages)
    A dramatic telling of how animals protect themselves,
this beautiful book provides a thumbnail sketch of pond life.
The wise old bullfrog suns himself on a rock, unaware of the
approach of the hungry heron.   He escapes just in time, for
he is very wise to the ways of the pond, which is "why he
has lived so long."

Activity--Primary

To promote attentive listening, ask the children to
count the number of insects, birds, animals and fish that are
named in the story.   How many names can they remember?
Ask the librarian to gather a collection of easy non-fiction
books on pond or forest creatures for the classroom reading
table.   Children should report orally on those that they read.
If available, obtain Encyclopaedia Britannica's World of Animals tape/book series and allow the children to spend time
listening to the tapes and following the texts.

Activity--Intermediate

This story might be read twice to the class.   The
first reading will tell the story and capture the beauty of the
language.   The second reading will give students a chance to
note all fifteen creatures that live around the pond.   Let each
student choose one living thing from the book (plant or animal) and find out more about it.   Illustrations and information can be posted on the bulletin board or compiled into a
class book on pond life.

Activities for the Very Youngest

In using the book with a pre-school or kindergarten
class, ditto masters can be made of the following illustrations.

Children will enjoy cutting out, coloring and using their own bookmark characters from the story, and the "Something's Missing" page will provide the teacher with a good check of the children's perception of the illustrations from the story. Most children should not need to see the illustrations again in order to add the missing part to the animals pictured on the ditto page. Children who do need to consult the illustrations, however, should be allowed to do so.

Gay, Zhenya. The Nicest Time of the Year. Illus. by the author. Viking Press, 1969. (K-2)
     A walk with a grown-up in early morning or evening in springtime may reveal a series of discoveries of newborn animals and birds. For the very youngest, these lovely illustrations will evoke a feeling of reverence for all of life and for the renewal of many species in spring.

SOMETHING'S MISSING

Activity

     Reading the book aloud will whet appetites for an im-
mediate nature walk, during which all living things discovered
can be noted and talked about upon return to the classroom.
Each child could make a picture of some living creature seen
(insect, bird or animal) to decorate the classroom walls or
bulletin board or windows with signs of spring.

Gay, Zhenya. Small One. Illus. by the author. Viking,
    1958. (K-2)
     Small One, a baby rabbit, knows that he is supposed
to stay hidden under the bramble bush with his brothers and
sisters while his mother is away. But after he mistakes the
thump of an acorn on the ground for his mother's "come-out"
signal, he enjoys his freedom so much and wanders so far
away from the bramble bush that he gets lost. After a
dangerous encounter with a fox, Small One is found by his
mother, who punishes him for disobeying (as any mother
would). Small One doesn't mind, however, for he is relieved to be back safe and sound with his family.

Activity

     Discuss with the children the dangers which face all
types of young wildlife in growing to maturity. What other
dangers might a small rabbit face, in addition to the fox?
What dangers might baby birds face in the springtime? Ask
the children if they have any ideas about what can be done
to protect wildlife? An invitation to the local conservation
groups in your area might result in a worthwhile sharing of
ideas between speaker and children.

Georgiou, Constantine. The Nest. Illus. by Bethany Tudor.
    Harvey House, 1972. (K-2)
     This is a simple retelling of how a robin builds her
nest in an apple tree. She fashions the nest with strong
twigs and lines it with fluff from a rabbit's tail. She plucks
wool from a lamb to tuck in the nest to keep it warm and
dry. Soon she lays five eggs and keeps them warm and dry
with her body through wind and cold and rain until the eggs
hatch. The simple text and clear illustrations should create
an interest among children about birds and their nests, and
lead to discoveries about the birds they see around their
homes in the spring.

Activity

     Before presenting the book, talk with an upper grade
teacher about the possibility of having older students do pencil sketches of different types of birds' nests.   Many excellent books are available on this subject and students should
be able to locate illustrations from which to make their drawings in books in the school or public library.   After presenting the book, display the drawings on the bulletin board with
the caption, "Who Lives Here?"   Students may visit the library individually or in small groups to find books on birds'
nests and try to identify the pictures.   Students' own drawings of the birds which belong to the various kinds of nests
can be posted beside the pictures of the nests.

Hader, Berta and Elmer.   Two Is Company, Three's a Crowd.
     Macmillan, 1965.   (2-4)
     Each year Big John and his wife Annabelle welcomed
the geese who stopped at the farm pond on their way to their
summer home in the north.   One year a goose and her mate
did not continue the journey with the others, so John and
Annabelle fed them through the summer with corn and bar-
ley.   In the fall the geese left but the next spring they returned, bringing many other geese with them.   None of the
geese left that spring, and each spring that followed saw more
and more geese arrive, until the farm was covered with
hundreds of birds.   Eventually the land around the farm was
made a waterfowl refuge and the geese were protected and
cared for forever after.   The story is based on an actual
event.

Activity

     Students may be interested in finding out more about
the migration of geese, where bird sanctuaries and waterfowl
refuges are located in the United States, and what birds are
in danger of becoming extinct.   If there is such a sanctuary
or refuge near your school, this book would serve as an
ideal springboard for a field trip.   Have students observe
birds around their school and home.   Each child can keep a
notebook about the birds seen and use the school library to
locate information about the birds.

Heyward, DuBose.   The Country Bunny and the Little Gold
     Shoes.   Illus. by Marjorie Flack.   Houghton-Mifflin,

1939.   (K-3)
     In this well-loved tale, five Easter bunnies deliver
eggs all over the world between Easter Eve and Easter morning.   They are chosen because of their kindness, swiftness
and wisdom.   A little brown country bunny longed to grow up
and be one of the Easter bunnies but she was scoffed at by
the white rabbits and the jack rabbits.   She grew up, married and eventually had twenty-one little cottontail babies.
She trained them so beautifully that when Grandfather Bunny
had to choose a replacement bunny for the Easter deliveries,
he chose her for being so clever, as well as kind, wise and
swift.   She was given a beautiful egg to deliver to a sick
child on the top of a snowy mountain and because of her courage in making the journey, she was rewarded with a pair of
beautiful gold shoes which enabled her to carry out her task.

Activities

1)   This is a delightful story for the classroom to dramatize
out on the playground where they can hop without restraint.
A narrator should be chosen to set the scene and the fun begins when the bunnies all gather on the great lawn of Grandfather Bunny.   As Mother Bunny calls them up two by two,
she introduces them with a description ("These are my sweep-
ers, etc.") and pairs of "bunnies" can pantomime their activity.   The climax of the performance might be the taking
of a special Easter basket to a nursing home or other place
of special need.   Then ALL the children can be the special-
ly chosen Easter bunnies!

2)   This story might be introduced several weeks before Easter and the children encouraged to "try out" for being one of
the five Easter Bunnies.   There could be a hopping race one
week, a broad jumping contest on another, and throughout, a
place to record incidences of kindness, wisdom and courage.
The record might be similar to the following:

Names	Kindness rendered	Hopping	Broad- jumping	Wisdom	Courage
Anne	X	X		XX	
Peter		X	X		
Charles			X	X	X

(Note: Small eggs might be drawn instead of Xs)

All of the children might take part in creating the
beautiful Easter basket mentioned previously (to be taken to
a nursing home or a home with special needs).   When the
final tally is made, the five who scored the highest total can
be the ones to deliver the basket.   The columns "kindness"
and "courage" give those children who are not scholars or
athletes an equal opportunity to excel, so be sure to notice
their good deeds!

Hoban, Russell.   Egg Thoughts and Other Frances Songs.
    Illus. by Lillian Hoban.   Harper & Row, 1972.   (all
    ages)
        The charming and funny rhymes shared by the little
badger, Frances, will be understood by children who have
had similar reactions.   Eggs and little sisters and chocolate
turn up in commonplace situations which all will recognize.
From homework to friendship, Frances speaks to the child
in anyone.

Activity

        The very first "Egg Thoughts" will encourage children
to write their own poem about some food which is not their
favorite.   Suggest that they entitle a rhyme "Broccoli
Thoughts" or "Mashed Potato Thoughts," and some strong-
feeling writers in your classroom may outdo Frances.

House, Charles.   The Lonesome Egg.   Illus. by Nola Lang-
    ner.   W. W. Norton Co., 1968.   (1-4)
        Billy found an egg on the forest floor.   He didn't know
what it belonged to, so he thought of making a nest for it
and putting it in his own collection.   But a mother bird might
be looking for it!   So he researched all the sizes and colors
of eggs of the birds in his community, yet couldn't find out
what it could possibly be.   One day, as he was watching the
egg, it hatched.   Out crawled a baby turtle!   Billy had
learned a great deal and had added 32 used-up egg shells
from many different birds and one turtle to his museum collection.

Activity

        When reading this aloud, stop when the egg is about
to hatch and let the children guess what it might contain.   A
study of bird, snake and turtle eggs could be initiated in the

spring after reading this book.   An egg chart showing the different sizes and shapes and colors could be made by the
children, so that egg shells found on nature walks may be
identified.   Stress that only egg shells are to be searched
for.   Unhatched eggs and the nests of birds should not be
touched.

Hutchins, Pat.   Rosie's Walk.   Ill. by the author.   Macmil-
     lan, 1968.   (all ages)
     Rosie, the hen, takes a walk around the farm.   The
fox sees Rosie's walk as a perfect opportunity to have a
plump, juicy hen for supper.   Unaware that she is being followed, Rosie leads the fox from one disaster to another, until finally he is chased by a swarm of bees and gives up his
prey entirely.   Rosie, never knowing all of the terrible
things that have happened to the fox, arrives back in time
for dinner.

Activity

     This hilarious story is a perfect vehicle for dramatic
play.   Wait for a sunny day and a time when the playground
is not busy to present the story.   In addition to the parts of
Rosie and the fox, have the children discuss the other farm
animals which might be present and allow the children to
choose the animal they want to be.   As the story is acted
out (without dialogue), various children can take turns in
acting out the parts of Rosie and the fox.   A word of caution: be sure that the children distinguish between dramatic
play and a too realistic reenactment of the story.   The
"swarm of bees," in particular, might get a bit carried
away in their parts without such a discussion.

Hutchins, Pat.   The Wind Blew.   Illus. by the author.   Mac-
     millan, 1974.   (all ages)
     A funny story, told in verse, of what happened in a
town one day when the wind blew.   It blew an umbrella inside out, caught up a balloon, a hat, a kite, a shirt, a
hankie, a wig, letters and a flag, and all of the people who
were carrying these things are in hot pursuit of them as the
wind tosses them higher and higher in the air.   Finally, "It
sent the newspapers fluttering round, then, tired of the things
it found, it mixed them up and threw them down ... and blew
away to sea. "

Activity

The wind in this story caused problems for a number
of people.   Ask the children if they can think of at least one
useful purpose of the wind.   Caution them to keep their
thought a secret and encourage them to illustrate their idea.
A delightful bulletin board of the children's drawings, entitled
"We Need Wind," can result.   Ideas will probably range from
the drying of clothes on a clothesline, to windmills, to, perhaps, the blowing away of ozone pollution over a city in the
drawings of more astute youngsters.

Ipcar, Dahlov.   The Wonderful Egg.   Illus. by the author.
     Doubleday, 1958.   (1-3)
     A story about a very different kind of egg that will
keep the reader (or listener) guessing to the end.   This particular egg sat in a "blue-green mossy nest" in a jungle one
hundred million years ago.   Guesses as to what will hatch
from the egg include dinosaurs, sea serpents and flying rep-
tiles.   But when the egg does hatch, out comes the very
first bird the world has ever known!   The book contains a
chart of dinosaurs with their sizes and pronunciation of their
names.

Activity

What can hatch from an egg other than a bird?   This
question might lead young researchers on an interesting adventure in the school library.   With the help of the librarian,
books on eggs can be located and studied.   Students will
quickly discover that both snakes (some species) and turtles
come from eggs, and perhaps will think of investigating insect eggs.   The research group can report its findings to
the class, showing the illustrations in those books they have
located which led to their findings.

Keats, Ezra Jack.   Jennie's Hat.   Illus. by the author.
     Harper and Row, 1966.   (K-2)
     Jennie's aunt sent her a new hat.   Jennie was quite
excited about it until she opened the box and saw that it
was quite a plain hat.   Jennie could not help but wish that
her hat were more like the beautiful creations she saw the
ladies wearing at church.   Then, one Sunday on her way
home from church, Jennie's wish came true as her friends,
the birds, began bringing all sorts of things, from flowers

to greeting cards, and putting them on Jennie's hat.   The
plain straw hat became a hat never to be forgotten!

Activity

Let the class as a whole design a hat for the teacher
to wear for a day! Bring to school an old straw hat (fem-
inine style if for a female teacher or "fishing hat" style if
for a male teacher). Let the children decide what could be
added to the hat to make it a true creation that the teacher
will be proud to wear. This may require considerable discussion. Using the scrap box in the classroom or materials
brought from home, each child should make a contribution to
the hat. When the hat has been completed, the teacher
MUST wear it for a day to make the project a success!

Kuskin, Karla.   The Bear Who Saw the Spring.   Illus. by
        the author.   Harper & Row, 1961.   (K-2)
        This book of the four seasons begins when bear meets
a puppy who "is very young and small and he has not seen
much at all." Since bear is much older than the puppy, he
tells the little dog all about spring, with its green grass,
buds, leaves, nests, birds, eggs, tadpoles, flowers and
caterpillars. Told in lilting verse, this delightful introduction to the spring season should start children thinking about
signs of spring and build an awareness of those signs to
watch for as they play out of doors.

Activity

Take a "dumb naturalist" walk with the class looking
for and collecting signs of spring. On this short walk (even
a corner of the schoolyard can prove interesting) no one can
talk, but each must show his or her partner something interesting he or she has discovered. If possible, let each student bring back three interesting things--this might be rocks,
bits of wood, leaves or weeds (use caution in selection).
On return to the class, take time to look over the "finds."
If magnifying glasses are available, use them. There are
many ways these treasures can be used. Press all leaves
and weeds between catalog pages or dry newspapers and
stack heavy objects on them. When pressed pieces are completely dried, mount them on construction paper backgrounds
with white glue.
        Small pebbles can be arranged into a small mosaic or
placed in a group on a piece of wood. Rocks can become

FROM A NATURALISTS
WALK

"pets" or be painted with watercolor; or a worried face can
be painted on a rock so that it can do your worrying for
you!

Lund, Doris. Attic of the Wind. Illus. by Ati Forbert.
     Parents Magazine Press, 1966. (all ages)
     This beautifully illustrated poem is filled with imagina-
tion and imagery. "What happens to things that blow away?"
Bubbles, snowflakes, flower petals, butterflies, feathers,
balloons, kites and a host of other things are stored in the
"attic of the wind," waiting to be discovered.

Activity--Primary

     Obtain the beautifully done Weston Woods filmstrip of
Attic of the Wind to show to primary students. Discuss with
the children both the good and not so good aspects of the
wind. Answers might range from "it helps me fly my kite"
to "it tangles my hair. "

Activity--Intermediate

     Older students will be surprised at the information
they discover about wind if a short research project is undertaken on the subject. Either working singly or in small
groups, have the children develop five questions to be answered about wind. Sample questions might be: Does a
brisk wind always indicate a change in weather? Does wind
serve any useful purpose? If so, what? What causes wind?
Let students report their findings to the class.

McCloskey, Robert. Make Way for Ducklings. Illus. by the
     author. Viking Press, 1941. (K-2)
     Mr. and Mrs. Mallard find a new home for their eight
newly hatched ducklings. The home is located in a nice pond
in a public garden right in the middle of Boston. The problem of getting the ducklings through the busy city traffic to
the pond is solved with the help of the Boston Police Force.
A well-loved classic, beautifully told and illustrated.

Activity

     Discuss with the class the different environments
needed for the birds and animals that are most often fea-
tured at Easter time--ducks, chicks, bunnies. Help the chil-

dren to see what might happen to these animals if one tried
to make house pets of them. If possible, invite a representative of the local animal protection society to come to
the class and talk with the children about the problem of trying to make pets of ducks, rabbits or chickens.

Martin, Bill, Jr. I Paint the Joy of a Flower. Holt, Rine-
     hart & Winston, 1970. (all ages)
     This is a little book of paintings by sixteen artists.
Each painting is captioned with one line of a tone poem to
reflect the variety of moods and many types of beauty found
in nature. It is a book which should be available in the classroom for children to browse through and enjoy.

Activity

     If the library has sets of art prints, picture sets or
study prints, borrow those which have spring themes to display in the classroom. Ask each child to choose his favorite picture and write a sentence about it which begins: "This
picture reminds me of _____." Encourage imaginative
writing rather than literal descriptions. A picture of a gey-
ser, for example, reminded one child of "A genie coming
out of a bottle." When good sentences are developed they
can be expanded into descriptive paragraphs, and from that
point into original stories.

Miles, Miska. Rabbit Garden. Illus. by John Schoenherr.
     Little-Brown, 1967. (1-3)
     A small rabbit flees from the men and machines that
are tearing up the meadow and takes refuge in a quiet garden
near a house. He soon discovers that he is not alone and
that among the other creatures who feed and rest in the garden are jays, a spider, a wounded dove, sparrows, a lady
bug, a possum, a mole and a mouse. Dangers lurk there,
too, in the form of a dog and a cat, but as time passes, the
rabbit becomes larger and braver and claims the garden as
his own.

Activity

     Children will enjoy (and learn much from) creating
their own "Rabbit Garden" bulletin board or mural in the
classroom. A springtime background can be made by making
tall grass shapes cut from both construction paper and wall-

paper books and placing them on a blue background. Add cut
paper garden creatures and flowers as well as vegetables.
Let a committee make the background and the rest of the
class add large-sized objects (animals, birds, insects, flowers, vegetables, etc.) which would be found in a typical garden. These can be cut from large poster paper, outlined in
black felt marker and appropriately painted or colored before
being placed on the spring background.

Milhous, Katherine. The Egg Tree. Illus. by the author.
     Scribner's, 1950. (all ages)
     The children of a Pennsylvania Dutch farm have an
Easter egg hunt. Little Katy finds no eggs until she discovers a hat in the attic which is filled with beautifully painted
hollow ones. They had been made years before and Grandmom had forgotten them. She strung them each with a thread
and hung them onto a little bare branched tree. Thus began
the family tradition of painting eggs for the egg tree each
Easter. The book is filled with authentic old country designs
and motifs.

Activity

     What class of children would not want to create its
own beautiful egg tree after reading this little classic? Children can learn to blow out the insides of an egg by pricking
a hole in each end. This project might be started long before Easter so that a large collection can be ready for painting as the holiday approaches. A large dead tree can be
secured in a bucket of sand (or cement) and the eggs hung
as they are decorated. Other classes can be invited to see
the finished egg tree and be offered a rabbit cookie as baked
by Grandmom. An Easter song learned and sung by the
class makes a happy addition to the sharing time.

Patterson, Lillie. Easter. Illus. by Kelly Oeschsli. Gar-
     rard, 1966. (all ages)
     This easy-to-read book is an excellent source of in-
formation about Easter, its origin, and the customs and folklore which surround the holiday. Beginning with an explanation of the spring festival celebrations of pre-Christian days,
the author explains how these early celebrations evolved into
the celebration of Easter as we know it today. Chapter head-
ings reveal the completeness of content: Sunday of Joy, Eggs
and Rabbits, Gifts and Greetings, Easter Foods, Symbols and
Customs, and Easter in Legend, Poetry and Song.

Barth, Edna. Lilies, Rabbits and Painted Eggs. Illus. by
  Ursula Arndt. The Seabury Press, 1970. (4-6)
    This story of Easter symbols traces the many cus-
toms and traditions of Easter as they are found all over the
world, from early pagan rites to the present-day celebrations. The author gives a wealth of background information
on such well-known Easter symbols as sunrise, fire, candlelight, eggs, chickens, fireworks, animals, foods, colors,
bells plants and clothing. The book is indexed so that young
researchers should have no difficulty in using it to locate information on a particular place or custom. The book is an
excellent source of carefully researched information on the
holiday.

Activities

    Both of these books can be used by student research-
ers who are looking for information about Easter. Students
might enjoy compiling their own book of Easter symbols.
Let each member of the class choose a letter (perhaps the
first letter of his or her last name) and find and read about
an Easter symbol or custom which begins with that letter.
(Since X and Z and Q might be difficult to find, these letters should not be assigned.) After the student has located
the information, he or she can illustrate the symbol or custom and include the name and a brief explanation of the custom at the top or bottom of the paper. The papers can be
laminated and put together with metal rings to become an
ABC Book of Easter Customs. Be sure one page of the book
contains all of the authors' names!

EASTER SCRAMBLE

    In the word scramble below are 16 Easter-related
words or phrases. Can you find them?

(For the teacher) Here are the words
to be found (some appear twice)

GXOSUNDAYOFJOY
RSBJKLILYNDELM
EVPCJYUPASQUAD
ADARBBFAGNMMMC   Sunday of Joy   Easter
TKQOEEASTERGBH   Great Day   egg
DCUSLIJCFGRATI   Glad Day   lamb
ATESLLOUOGRBFC   Feast of Flowers   cross
YESETSPASENOPK   Pasqua   rabbit
XGLADDAYLAMBEE   Pascua   bells
RTRABBITCROSSN   Pasques   chickens
FEASTOFFLOWERS   Pasen   lily

All terms in the word scramble above can be found in Lillie
Patterson's Easter or Edna Barth's Lilies, Rabbits and
Painted Eggs.

Politi, Leo. Song of the Swallows. Illus. by the author.
      Scribner's, 1949. (all ages)
      A charming story of the mission country of California
is set in the town of Capistrano where little Juan helps the
old gardener and bell ringer of the Mission of San Juan Capistrano. Julian tells Juan of the early mission days and of
the swallows who return each spring to nest at the mission.
The birds leave in late summer and return on St. Joseph's
Day. No one can explain where they go or how they know
to return each spring. Great joy comes to Juan when the
garden he has prepared for the swallows is chosen by a
nesting pair.

Activity--Primary

      What fun it will be to have the swallows arrive in the
classroom in time for Easter! Prepare a simple pattern on
a ditto master similar to the one illustrated. Give each
child a copy. Children will need crayons, scissors and a
length of string (about 12"). Instruct children to color the
body and the wings of the bird. Cut out the bird and the
slot for the wings on the heavy black lines. Cut out the
wings. Fold the wings on the dotted line like a fan. Insert
the wings into the slot in the bird. Tie a string through the
dot in the bird's back and hang.

Activity--Intermediate

      Some students may be interested in following up on a
study of migration to see what the latest research has to say
about this remarkable instinct of birds. Others could do
further research on the early history of California and the
founding of the missions. The whole class could make a project in early spring (if a small plot of ground is available)
of creating a garden of plants which attract birds and perhaps
adding a bird bath for drinking and bathing. Student researchers can record which birds come to the "garden." A field
trip to find and watch, (not touch!) nests is always exciting
in the spring. Local chapters of the Sierra Club, Audubon
Society or Natural History Societies are good sources for
speakers and for information if you are not aware of what is
available in your area.

Song of the Swallows
  by Leo Politi

Mobile

Color the body and wings of the bird.

Cut out the bird and the slot for the wings on the heavy
black lines.

Wings

Cut out the wings.

Fold the wings on
the dotted lines like
a fan.

Insert wings into
the slot in the
bird.

Tie a string
through the dot
on the bird's
back and hang.

Potter, Beatrix. The Tale of Peter Rabbit. Illus. by the
    author. Frederick Warne & Co. , n.d. (K-2)
        This beloved story of Flopsy, Mopsy, Cotton-Tail and
Peter, who lived with their mother "underneath the root of
a very big fir tree," is a classic in children's literature.
Disobedient Peter crawls under the gate into Mr. McGregor's
garden and feasts on vegetables until the farmer takes off
after him.   The long and frightening chase ends as Peter arrives home and is put to bed with a dose of camomile tea.
Good little Flopsy, Mopsy and Cotton-Tail have bread and
milk and blackberries for their supper.

Activity

        One first grade gave a delightful Eastertime perform-
ance of this story set to the music and song of "Here Comes
Peter Cottontail. " All of the children participated.   Some
were cabbages, some parsley, and some radishes, all neatly
planted in rows.   Peter left home and family and hopped up
and down the rows in time to the music, nibbling here and
there, until spotted by Mr. McGregor who gave him a merry chase.   The teacher taught all of the vegetables as well
as the main characters a simple dance which wound up the
performance.   Flopsy, Mopsy and Cotton-Tail left their
blackberry picking to join in.
        Simple suggestions for costumes make this a fun ac-
tivity for children.   Painted-on whiskers and paper ears are
enough for the rabbits.   Green construction paper hats for
the cabbages and red for the radishes make the effect of a
garden.   This home-done production may not be as magnificent as the British Ballet movie version, but will be unforgettable to performers and parents.

Stone, Harris A. The Last Free Bird. Illus. by Sheila
    Heins. Prentice-Hall, 1967.   (all ages)
        "Once we were many living in quiet valleys and green
fields" and "I am the last free bird" are the opening and
closing lines of this dramatic and thoughtful picture book.
The opening illustrations of bubbling brooks, forests and
marshlands gradually give way to towns, cities and monstrous
factories with smoke stacks which "spilled and spewed and
changed the world. " No reader could fail to see the effect
of technology on man's environment.

Activity--Primary

        Ask primary children to discover what birds can be

found around their homes. The class might start a collection of pictures (either gathered or drawn by students) of
birds native to their locale. Young researchers, with the
help of the librarian, might want to find out what can be
done to keep the birds in the community.

Activity--Intermediate

        This simple book has three distinct parts, the beauty
and freedom of nature, the transition to modern technology,
and the desperation of the wild birds as they seek a place to
nest. The moods felt by the reader as he or she moves
from one part to another can be expressed through music.
If a record collection is available ask a group of students to
find music they feel best expresses the mood of each part of
the story. They should practice reading the story and read
it aloud to the class with the appropriate background music.

Thayer, Jane. The Horse with the Easter Bonnet. Illus. by
    Jay Hyde Barnum. Morrow, 1953. (K-3)
        Mr. O'Flaherty didn't get any business with his car-
riage because Josie, his horse, stood with her head hanging
low. People paid for other carriages to take them on rides
through the park, but Josie was underfed and slow--that is,
until an Easter bonnet landed one day right at her feet. She
tried to eat the flowers but Mr. O'Flaherty put the hat on
her head. Josie was delighted and trotted with her head
high. Business picked up immediately and a good dinner was
had that night.

Activity

        How about a hat-decorating contest? Pass out paper
plates to which ribbons or string can be attached for tying
under the chin, then let the children's creativity take over.
They can make paper flowers, flags, paint or crayon designs
on the plate, add streamers or whatever they might find at
home or in the classroom scrap box. Encourage imaginations to soar.

Tresselt, Alvin. The World in the Candy Egg. Illus. by
    Roger Duvoisin. Lothrop, Lee & Shepard, 1967. (all
    ages)
        A magical, make-believe world comes alive inside a
candy egg. Houses, people at work, animals, birds, flowers

and all sorts of colorful sights await one fortunate enough to
peek inside the egg. When the egg is placed in a box the
candy world is covered with darkness and all motion stops,
only to begin again when a new owner of the egg lifts it from
its wrappings to be touched by the bright sunlight. Lyrical,
descriptive prose and brilliantly colored illustrations do indeed bring alive the world in the candy egg.

Activity

     Let the children create their own egg worlds by mak-
ing large papier-maché eggs, cutting off one end and constructing a scene inside. Materials needed are oval shaped
balloons, wallpaper paste and strips of newspaper. Blow up
the balloon and tie the end so that air will not escape. One
person should hold the balloon while another applies newspaper strips which have been dipped in wallpaper paste. Six
to eight layers of strips are needed. Allow the figure to dry
completely before painting the outside, clipping off one end,
removing the balloon and building a scene inside. Small,
simple cardboard figures can be used. (If the painting of
the inside of the egg is desired, spray paint can be used
and allowed to dry before figures are added.) Children may
want to write stories about the egg worlds they have created
and tell the stories to the class as they show their eggs.

Williams, Margery. The Velveteen Rabbit. Illus. by Nichol-
    son. Doubleday, 1958. (all ages)
    A classic and sensitive story about how toys become
real to their owners. A beloved stuffed rabbit is a little
boy's constant companion. He learns from another toy, the
skin horse, about becoming real. "Real isn't how you are
made. It's a thing that happens to you. When a child loves
you for a long, long time, not just to play with but REALLY
loves you, then you become real." The rabbit sadly learns
that one doesn't become "real" until "most of your hair has
been loved off, and your eyes drop out and you get loose in
the joints and very shabby." After the little boy has a bout
with scarlet fever, all of his toys are taken outside to be
burned. The battered velveteen rabbit sheds a tear over his
fate, but the magic which results from his real tear turns
him into a real rabbit forever and ever.

Activity

     Ask the children if they ever had an especially loved

toy which became real. Find out if they still have, at home,
such a beloved toy tucked away in a closet, which they could
bring to school. These old friends could sit along the edge
of a table or chalkboard. If a child no longer has the toy
which meant the most to him, he might draw a picture of it
and put it beside the others. Give each child an opportunity
to tell how his toy became real, when it happened and how
it happened. Some children might rather write the story,
which could then be posted beside the toy or picture. Help
the children to see the fun of reminiscing, and of using their
imaginations. To help the class get started, the teacher
might be the first to share memories of a beloved plaything.

For older classes a great creative writing project
could be initiated on the topic of "What became of my Teddy
Bear?" (or bridedoll, or bulldozer or whiskered mouse).
Encourage the children to let their imaginations run freely
for delightful and unselfconscious stories.

Young, Miriam. Miss Suzy's Easter Surprise. Illus. by
Arnold Lobel. Parents Magazine Press, 1972. (K-3)
Miss Suzy Squirrel is finding bits and pieces from nature to trim her new Easter bonnet when a storm blows a
tree down, causing four baby squirrels to become homeless.
Miss Suzy forgets her usual Easter projects in making a new
home for the orphans and finally cuts up her bonnet to make
Easter baskets for them. She postpones returning to her beloved home at the top of an oak tree until the little squirrels
have been raised. Without being "preachy" this story is an
effective lesson in love and kindness.

Activity

Take your class on a field trip to the country or to
a nearby park where they can create their own original
Easter baskets from leaves and grass, wildflowers and weeds.
Take along some old bread or sandwich scraps so that the
children can fill their baskets with tidbits to leave for the
birds and animals. If seeds and unpopped corn are available,
they could be taken, too. Alert the children ahead of time
so that animal edibles can be saved. This can provide an
effective lesson in the idea that one species' "garbage" can
be another's Easter feast!

SPRING BIRTHDAYS

Spring is a delightful time to consider one or more
birthday parties for a favorite author. What fun to start the
first day of spring with a birthday party for Phyllis McGinley (3/21/05), or Eleanor Cameron (3/23/12). Invitations
to a party in honor of Mrs. Cameron might be shaped like
mushrooms (from The Wonderful Flight to the Mushroom
Planet) or space ships. Decorations can be bright mobiles
of characters from her books or a mural or posters depicting scenes from the works of this favorite author. Activities
can be similar to those suggested for Fall Birthdays or new
activities can be added. Some suggestions are:

1. To Tell the Truth. Select one title by the author and
    choose a panel of three students, one of whom has read
    the book and the other two who have not. Students in
    the class can ask questions of the panel members, try-
    ing to ascertain which student on the panel has actually
    read the book. Questioners can be from the entire class
    or made up of a panel of students who have read the
    book. A time-limit for guessing the "real reader" can
    be set.

2. New words from the author's name. Write the author's
    full name on the chalkboard. Allow the students five
    minutes to see how many new words they can make from
    the letters in the author's name. If prizes are desir-
    able for the winner(s), consider paperback copies of the
    author's books.

3. Hidden Book Titles. Write a story or have the children
    write their own stories, using as many of the titles of
    books by one author as they can. If the teacher writes
    the story, it can be duplicated for the class. If each
    student writes a story, these can be given to members
    of the visiting class to use in finding the hidden titles.
    A sample story using titles by Leo Lionni (5/5/10) fol-
    lows. Titles would NOT be underlined on the copy given
    to students.

Colors, Colors Everywhere!

My name is Frederick. I live in the biggest
house in the world. Outside my house in the rab-

bit garden stands the alphabet tree which has little
blue and little yellow leaves.   The greentail mouse
likes to eat them.   In front of my house is a beautiful lake and on my beach there are many pebbles.
Every morning Swimmy, my favorite fish, swims
inch by inch up to the alphabet tree, for he would
like to have a color of his own.   But before he
can get close he is frightened away by Theodore
and the talking mushroom.   "Well," says Swimmy,
"fish is fish and we belong in the water so I guess
I'll leave the tree for Theodore and Alexander and
the wind up mouse to play under.

A partial listing of authors with spring birthdays:

March

Eleanor Cameron 3/23/12
Phyllis McGinley 3/21/05
Barbara Byfield 3/28/30

April

Glen Rounds 4/4/06
Beverly Cleary 4/12/16
Harold Keith 4/8/03
Jean Lee Latham 4/19/02
Jan Wahl 4/1/33
Evaline Ness 4/24/11

May

Tom Feelings 5/19/33
Leo Lionni 5/5/10
Elizabeth Coatsworth 5/3/93
Irene Hunt 5/18/07
Stephen Meader 5/2/92
Keith Robertson 5/9/14
Zilpha Snyder 5/11/27

June

Esther Forbes 6/18/91

HOLIDAY THRILLS YIELD STUDY SKILLS

Using Holiday Books to Promote
Independent Study Activities

One of the greatest gifts any educator can give to a child is to arm him or her with the skills necessary for life-long independent learning. The advent of instant technology and the speeded-up communications systems in today's world have created a society where the total accumulated knowledge of civilization doubles every generation. It seems obvious that not only is it impossible for one human mind to contain all pertinent knowledge but that the growth of knowledge makes much that is taught in the schools obsolete by the time a child has finished his or her formal education. Thus, teaching children HOW to learn assumes a role of major importance on today's educational scene.

No matter what skills it is necessary for students to acquire, certain basic guidelines must be uppermost in the mind of the teacher or librarian if any skill is to be successfully mastered. Foremost is the premise that the student must be motivated to want to acquire the skill, have a need for the skill and be given the opportunity to immediately apply the skill in a functional situation.

Holiday books can serve as perfect springboards to the development of independent study skills. The holiday itself is nearly always looked forward to eagerly, thus providing built-in motivation. Holiday activities which require research on the part of students nearly always result in a class sharing or using the data which is gathered. Thus, motivation, need and application all become a part of the holiday research activity.

It is important to note that the research project, whether undertaken by primary or intermediate students, does not always have to result in a written report of some

158

type. After a sharing of Hays' The Story of Valentine, a
Roman town can emerge as a table model only after considerable research has been done concerning the type of buildings found in Ancient Rome, the dress of the people, the
kinds of streets, means of transportation, etc.

Hoban's The Mole Family's Christmas can lead to a
search of books, newspapers and magazines by primary students to locate one animal characteristic and to draw a picture of a gift which would be suitable for that animal. (For
example, the student who discovers in Ranger Rick magazine
that snakes shed their skins once a year might draw a picture of an electric heater, or a new coat or some other object that would be suitable for a "naked" snake!)

Haley's Jack Jouett's Ride can lead to research on
how colonial leaders celebrated Halloween. Dalgliesh's The
Thanksgiving Story will stimulate children to want to find out
about ocean voyages in the 1600s and 1700s. What food was
taken along? What was the cargo? How long did a voyage
last? What were the dangers?

Information on Christmas Tree farms can be gathered
after sharing Brown's Little Fir Tree. Routes from Judea
to Rome can be located and traced as children enjoy The
Legend of Befana by Chafetz. Discovering the mythical "wee
people" of the world can be a fascinating activity as students
are introduced to Astrid Lindgren's The Tomten. The threat
to Alaskan wildlife will become more than just a newspaper
story to students who research this topic after reading Hader's
Reindeer Trail. An all-school program based on the Christmas scenes from the books in the "Little House" series by
Laura Ingalls Wilder will require much investigation of the
many aspects of pioneer life which are to be portrayed.

Certainly February birthdays of great Americans will
inspire students to learn more about Washington and Lincoln
and other great men who have been Presidents of the United
States. The list of books on the Presidents is endless and
every student can take part in such a research project since
titles can be found which are either broad or narrow in
scope, and easy or difficult in reading level.

The coming of spring and the celebration of spring
holidays can provide many research opportunities. Politi's
Song of the Swallows will interest intermediate students in
finding out more about the migration of birds and about the

establishment of the early Missions in California and the
Southwest. Primary children will have fun developing a chart
of sizes, shapes and colors of eggs which might be found in
their area in the spring after they have shared House's The
Lonesome Egg. The possibilities are endless and the re-
wards in students' increased skill development and knowledge
are great.

A Sample Research Project--Grades Two and Three

1. Share with the class either Harris's The Last Free Bird
    or Hader's Two Is Company, Three's a Crowd, or any
    other favorite book on birds. Prepare beforehand six or
    eight ditto masters which are outline drawings of birds
    usually found in your area. Perhaps the art teacher in
    the school would be willing to do this for you.

2. Follow the reading of the text with a class question-and-
    answer time. Is it possible that all birds might some-
    day disappear from the Earth? What birds can you name
    that are seen around your home or school? Where do
    they live? What do they eat? What can we do to help
    birds in the winter? In the summer? Distribute one of
    the outline drawings to each child (the same drawing to
    each).

3. As each child looks at the outline drawing, ask: "Would
    you like to color this bird? What color should it be?
    How can we find out? What else can we add to the pic-
    ture to show that we know other things about this bird?
    Children will suggest a nest (what kind, what shape?),
    eggs (how many?) food (what kind?), enemies (what are
    they?). As each suggestion is made, ask the class
    where the information might be found. Suggestions will
    probably range from volume B (for birds) in the ency-
    clopedia to books on birds. Stress that the first step
    must be to identify the bird. This identification will
    then give students the key word to search for in the card
    catalog, the index to a book on birds or the encyclopedia.
    As the children discover information about the bird they
    add this information to their pictures in the form of
    drawings. A nest can be added which is the proper
    shape, located in the proper place; the correct number
    of eggs can be drawn in the nest; food can be drawn in
    the bird's mouth; enemies can lurk nearby; and the bird
    should, of course, be named and colored correctly.

Children do not have to do all six or eight pictures.
Let each child work at his or her own pace. Be sure the
librarian is informed of the project in advance so that ample
materials can be placed on reserve for the class to use.
Finished drawings can be assembled in booklet form and children encouraged to take their booklets home and share their
new-found information with their parents.

Advantages of this type of project

The traditional method of assigning each child a topic
and asking the children to locate information on the topic in
the school library usually results in students obtaining the
nearest encyclopedia and copying down the first two or three
paragraphs of the article which is pertinent to their needs.
No real skills for independent study are involved. The above
method requires little writing but, at the same time, brings
into play nearly all of the skills which are essential to an independent study activity.

The student must first identify the bird. The encyclopedia will usually suffice for this. However, since few
school libraries contain 30 volume Bs of an encyclopedia,
many students will be forced to locate books on birds. This
requires using the card catalog, understanding subject cards
and call numbers, locating the bird books by call number,
using skimming skills to identify the bird, and using the indexes of a variety of books on birds to locate information on
a specific bird once it has been identified. In this case, information is recorded in the form of drawings.

Alternate Activity--Grade 3

Working closely with the school librarian, develop a
list of questions about birds. Use the bird books in your
school library for this purpose, basing one question on each
book. Be sure to choose books which cover a wide range of
reading levels. Examine the sample list of questions given
below. Note that numbers 1-7 give the page on which the
answer can be found. The reading level of these first seven
books is first and second grade. Students with reading diffi-
culties should be able to have a successful experience locating information in these first seven books. It is most important that all children have an opportunity to find success
in a research project, and the listing of questions in this way
provides for the student who is less talented academically.

Questions 8 through 21 are taken from books which are third grade reading level, and 22 through 24 are from books which are above third grade level. Stress that questions do not have to be answered in order. This will result in books being available to every child and these books can be exchanged with any other child as they are used. The only restriction would be to assure the availability of the first seven titles to those children who have special needs. At the completion of the project children can share their information with each other to see if their answers are similar (if not, is more research needed?), and can add this information to the earlier booklet done on birds.

Again, the search for specific information requires the child to locate key words in a question and to use indexes and skimming skills to find a particular answer. Through such a project, students should come to the realization that information on birds (or any other topic) can be found in a variety of sources and that one does not have to depend totally on the encyclopedia for answers!

WE LEARN ABOUT BIRDS

1. Which bird can see to fly at night? Friskey, The True Book of Birds We Know, page 22.

2. Do chickens have teeth? Darby, What Is a Chicken? page 30.

3. How many days does the mother hen sit on the eggs? Darby, What Is a Chicken? page 10.

4. What do the baby chicks eat? Darby, What Is a Chicken? page 20.

5. Which bird is big and blue with a black ring around its neck? Selsam, Tony's Birds, page 33.

6. Which bird has a call that sounds as though it is saying, "Teacher, Teacher, Teacher"? Selsam, Tony's Birds, page 58.

7. Name two birds that cannot fly. Friskey, The True Book of Birds We Know, page 40 and 41.

8. Does the male robin usually sit on the nest? Mason, Robins.

9. Name 3 birds that do not fly away in the winter.
    Ozone, Winter Tree Birds.

10. How many eggs does the mother hummingbird lay?
    John, Hummingbirds.

11. How fast can a duck fly? Palmer, Birds.

12. What does a robin use to make her nest? Wasson,
    Birds.

13. What does a duck have near its tail to make it water-
    proof? Goldin, Ducks Don't Get Wet.

14. Where does the meadowlark build her nest? Gans, It's
    Nesting Time.

15. How does a gull open a shell to get the meat inside it?
    Wright, Look at a Gull.

16. What does the Everglade kite use its long hooked beak
    for? Luce, Birds That Hunt.

17. What kind of food did they put on the porch to feed the
    birds in the winter? Garelick, Winter's Birds.

18. Of what family are cockatoos a member? Andrews,
    Birds.

19. Name two birds of the desert. Mathewson, The How
    and Why Wonder Book of Birds.

20. Where does the screech owl make its nest? Rand,
    Birds in Summer.

21. Why is the catbird called the catbird? Hausman, My
    Book About Birds.

---

22. What does the blue jay do to prepare for winter? May,
    A Book of American Birds.

23. What does the yellow warbler do when she finds a cow-
    bird's egg in her nest? Holden, The Ways of Nesting
    Birds.

24. Where do California condors nest? Do they use nest-
    ing materials? Hogner, Birds of Prey.

The Research Activity--Intermediate Grades

        Independent study activities for intermediate grades
can be successful if careful planning precedes such activities.

Students who pursue knowledge independently are able to support or deny existing concepts and develop new concepts through the use of a wide variety of print and nonprint materials. Cooperative planning of teacher and librarian is the key to success!

Steps in Successful Independent Study Activities

1. The teacher sets the goals and objectives to be achieved by students during a particular unit of work. (Student input into development of goals and objectives should be encouraged.)

2. A planning conference is held between the teacher and the librarian. The teacher gives the librarian the concepts to be developed during the unit of study, the topics and subtopics to be explored, and informs the librarian of students with special learning problems. Arrangements are made for the class to visit the center and meet with the librarian, who will introduce materials to be used during the study and stimulate interest in their use. If particular work/study skills need to be taught or reinforced for use during the research project, these can be reviewed or taught at this time.

3. Students in the classroom survey the topic as a whole (for example Hader's Reindeer Trail might interest the students in finding out more about disappearing Alaskan wildlife), and each child selects a topic of interest to explore (for example, one Alaskan animal). An alternate approach is to assign topics to small groups of students if committee work is preferred to individual work.

4. After the topic has been selected, and before visiting the library, students "brainstorm" both individually and in small groups to determine what is to be learned about the topic. (Habits of the Alaskan animal? Description? Habitat? Dangers to its disappearance as a species? etc.) QUESTIONS TO BE ANSWERED ARE LISTED. Key words are circled in each question. These steps are important in directing the students' thinking in a specific area, requiring the use of many sources (and practice in using an index and skimming skills), and in preventing the copying of large blocks of material from the encyclopedia.

5. Following the listing of questions, the student lists those
    sources of information most likely to have the answers
    for him.   These sources include every main idea or
    topic that can be found in the card catalog or indexes.
    (Example for the Alaskan wildlife study might be: the
    name of the animal chosen, name of specific area in
    Alaska where found, names of specific enemies when
    discovered, names and location of agencies set up to pro-
    tect wildlife, books on ecology, endangered species, con-
    servation, etc.) This is the real "think" phase of the
    activity and prevents aimless wandering and discourage-
    ment when the student begins his search for information
    in the library.

6. After topic, questions and sources are listed, the student
    begins his library search for information.   The informed
    librarian should always be ready to assist when difficulty
    arises in the search for information.   Skills for the suc-
    cessful location of materials that have been taught are
    actually learned at this phase of the project.

7. When specific answers are found, notes are made on sep-
    arate note cards, listing the information and its source.
    This will require one or more periods of classroom in-
    struction before students are ready to take notes on their
    own.

8. Notes are placed in outline form.   This might be a for-
    mal outline or an informal placing of main points in cor-
    rect sequence.

9. If a written report is to be the end result of the research
    activity, the finished product should be as correct as the
    student can make it.   This is the time for self-evaluation,
    when students work toward a well-done finished product.
    Now is the time for the teacher to emphasize grammar,
    punctuation, spelling, capitalization, etc.

10. Material does not always have to be presented as a writ-
    ten report! Students can be encouraged to present ma-
    terial in an interesting manner of their own choosing.
    In this unit the end result might be a "We were there"
    tape-script of the killing of baby seals; or an "ABC
    Write-On Filmstrip of Alaskan Wildlife," with each let-
    ter of the alphabet standing for an animal or some as-
    pect of animal preservation in Alaska; or demonstrations,
    dramatizations, visuals, puppets, debates, quizzes, etc.

A Final Note

The teacher must be sure that the student is ready
for each step before he proceeds to that step. All students
do not move through all of the steps at the same time.
While one group is taking notes, the teacher may be helping
a slower group develop their questions. When that group is
in the library locating information under the direction of the
librarian, the teacher may be having a lesson on outlining
with another group which has finished note-taking. The main
point to keep in mind is that the student who has mastered
the skills needed for each phase of the independent study activity is not likely to become discouraged. A form similar
to the one which follows can be used initially by students.
Once the process has been carried out and students are
familiar with the procedure, the form may not be necessary.
However, it does help to clarify student thinking, not only
about the information to be located but about the best reference sources to be used. The form also assists the librarian in helping the student who may run into problems in locating information.

                              Name _____

                        Research Report

TOPIC: _____

QUESTIONS THAT I WANT TO HAVE ANSWERED ABOUT
THIS TOPIC

1. _____

2. _____

3. _____

4. _____

5. _____

6. _____

7. _____

8. _____

SOURCES OF INFORMATION

A. Card catalog: Topic(s) _____

B. Encyclopedia: Topic(s) _____

C. Geographical Dictionary: Topic(s) _____

D. Famous First Facts: Topic(s) _____

E. Atlas: Topic(s) _____

F. Almanac: Topic(s) _____

G. Periodicals: Title(s) _____

H. Indexes: Topic(s) _____

I. Other:

      The role of holiday books as a motivating and stimu-
lating force in fostering independent study activities cannot
be denied. Good books release new energies in the minds
that absorb them. This energy radiates out in an ever-widen-
ing circle. Everything we read or experience is enhanced by
everything else we have read and experienced. We could
liken the consciousness of each child to a giant jigsaw puzzle, with pieces missing here and there. Each literary experience may fit a missing piece of understanding into the
whole until a solid and satisfying view is achieved. This is
truly the goal of Celebrating with Books !

INDEX TO TITLES, AUTHORS, ILLUSTRATORS